The Rock *of* Arles

Richard Klein

The Rock
of Arles

Duke University Press
Durham and London 2024

© 2024 Duke University Press
All rights reserved
Project Editor: Lisa Lawley | Designed by Aimee C. Harrison
Typeset in Garamond Premier Pro and Canela by Copperline
Book Services

Library of Congress Cataloging-in-Publication Data
Names: Klein, Richard, [date] author.
Title: The rock of Arles / Richard Klein.
Description: Durham : Duke University Press, 2024. |
Includes bibliographical references.
Identifiers: LCCN 2023020156 (print)
LCCN 2023020157 (ebook)
ISBN 9781478025726 (paperback)
ISBN 9781478020981 (hardcover)
ISBN 9781478027850 (ebook)
Subjects: LCSH: Arles (France)—History. | Arles (France)— History
—Philosophy. | BISAC: LITERARY CRITICISM / European / French
| LITERARY CRITICISM / Semiotics & Theory | LCGFT: Creative
nonfiction. | Counterfactual histories.
Classification: LCC DC801.A72 K545 2024 (print) |
LCC DC801.A72 (ebook) | DDC 944.9/18—dc23/eng/20230719 LC
record available at https://lccn.loc.gov/2023020156
LC ebook record available at https://lccn.loc.gov/2023020157

Cover art: Julie Seydoux, *Blue Mathematiques*, from the series
Genius Loci, 2020. Courtesy of the artist.

For Susan, my Rock

Contents

Author's Note ix

Prologue xi

I Urbs Dupleix 1

II Quid Obstat Fit in Via 19

III Colonia Julia Paterna Arelate 31

IV Venus Genetrix 45

V Urbs Genesii 54

VI Peri Tuché 70

VII Felix Carcar 86

VIII A Worthy Woman: [אשה הנוגה] 104

IX A Republic of Equals 121

Acknowledgments 145

Notes 149

Bibliography 153

Author's Note

I took as a model for this book *The Memoirs of Hadrian* by Marguerite Yource-nar, in which she imaginatively re-creates the mind and memories of the emperor Hadrian. The exhaustive research that enabled her to write the fiction was so rigorous that her novel has been cited by reputable historians of Rome for its evidence and hypotheses. In this (my much-less-accomplished) case, I have tried to imagine the vast history of Arles through the mind of a rock: the Rock of Arles. It was on this limestone eminence, rising up alongside the river Rhone, that the city was founded 2,600 years ago. The Rock of Arles has witnessed every instant of its rise and fall, and its memory is infallible. The Rock speaks in a voice like that of what the Romans called a *genius loci*, a genius or genie who incarnates—or more exactly, in this case, materializes—the spirit of the place.

The story told by the Rock differs sharply from the official histories; more polemical, philosophical, and dissident, it focuses narrowly on three of the most radical, revolutionary Arlesians whose lives and works have been largely forgotten in Arles and ignored in the wider world. It needs their lessons now more than ever. Each one belongs to a brilliant period in the history of the city. In the second century, Arles was the most important city in Gaul. In the thirteenth century, it was a great center for the earliest translations of ancient Greek texts, which sparked a renaissance of science and philosophy. In the eighteenth century, Arles, with its fierce division of Right and Left, royalists and Jacobins, *chiffonistes* and *monnaidiers*, was seen in Paris as a mirror image in miniature of the revolutionary struggle. Similarly, the story told here by the Rock of Arles can be taken to be a précis, an abridgment of the history of Europe from the imperial Roman conquest of Gaul to the rise and fall of feudal aristocracy, from the domination of the Church to the present representative democracy.

The work introduces three extraordinary Arlesians: Favorinus, an authentic philosopher and the greatest orator in Greek of his Hellenistic age; Ḳalonymus ben Ḳalonymus, a prolific translator of Arabic translations of Greek and a radical Hebrew poet; and Pierre-Antoine Antonelle, the first mayor of Arles, an aristocrat, a bloody revolutionary, and a great political thinker. They represent a dissident, freethinking current in the history of Arles that contests the reactionary conservative forces of the Church and the nobility that governed the city for fifteen hundred years.

This text is a fiction, which permits the author to make claims and assert opinions that a careful historian would never allow. It also authorizes invention: nothing in the text should be considered reliable. It represents a particular slant, a skewed vision, a jaundiced interpretation of the history of Arles with a view to its possible future—like all histories. As Emerson wrote in 1841, "There is properly no history: only biography." The Rock has a witty, ironic perspective on that history that aims to be erudite, opinionated, and entertaining.

Prologue

Ten years ago, my wife and I bought a house in Arles, at the far end of a street, la rue Porte de Laure, down which heroes of the arena, covered in blood and crowned with laurel wreaths, once were shouldered in triumph out of the city walls. One sweltering noon, not long ago, in the dog days of summer, when the heat of the Midi takes your breath away, I sought escape in the cellar of our house, which rests on ground dug into the Rock of Arles.

My cellar must have once been a place to dance or pray: its floor is randomly tessellated with multicolored pieces of mosaic. In the middle, however, is a circle of bare uneven ground from which the tiles have been removed, and it is there, on that spot, in the coolness of my wine cellar, that I settled my writing table. No sooner had I put down my computer when a drawly voice, muffled at first but more and more distinct, began to speak to me in a low rumbling, a half whisper that seemed to come from beneath my feet.

The voice said it was the Rock of Arles and that it often whispered to those who lived on its side—especially writers and artists—whenever there was some urgency, like now. The city is at a crossroads, it said, and the direction it takes will orient its history for the next hundred years. The Rock has a contrarian view of that history, but it needs a sympathetic amanuensis to convey it to the world, which needs it even more.

In the cool and the darkness, lit only by the light of the screen, I started taking notes as fast as I could. After each session—there were nine—I would rush upstairs and write down in English what I could remember verbatim in French, with the help of my notes. Later it occurred to me that I was doing exactly what Aulus Gellius used to do, after a banquet with Favorinus in Rome, except that

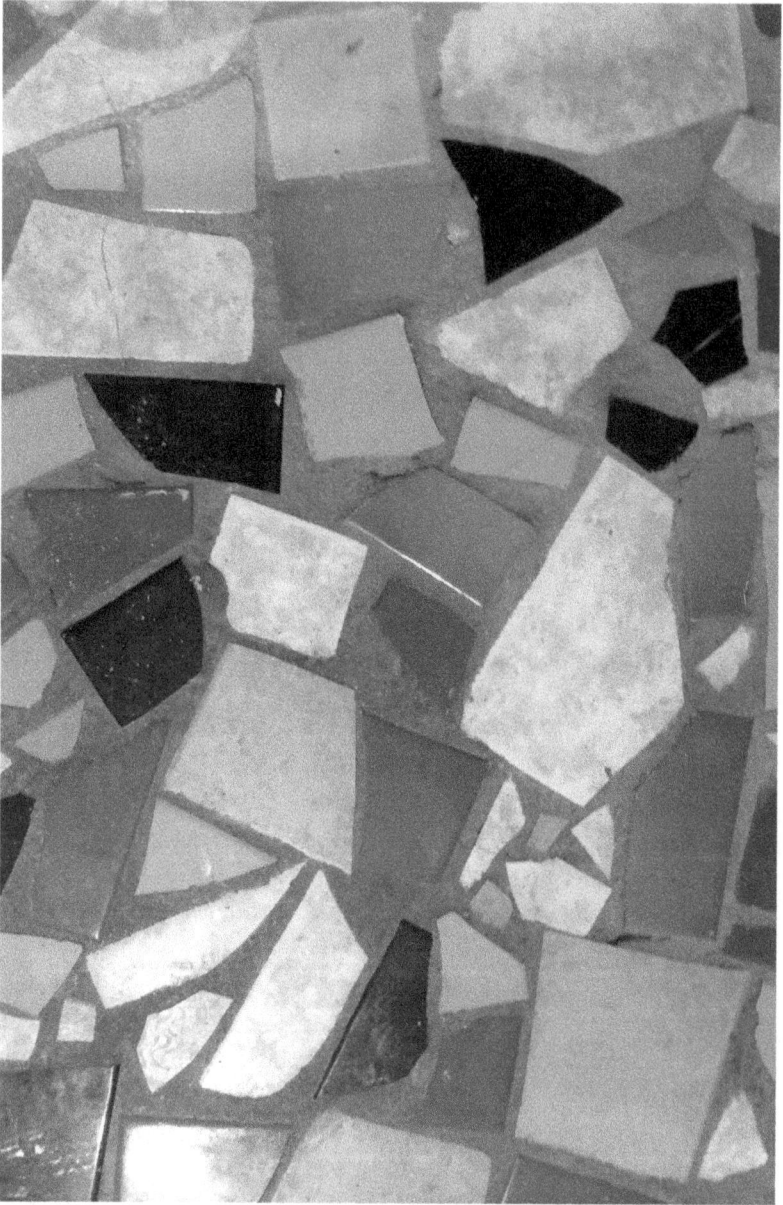

P.1. The tessellated floor of my cave

he had to run home to translate the stenographic notes he had taken of the philosopher's Greek into the equivalent literal Latin. Perhaps it won't then surprise the reader if occasionally the Rock of Arles sounds in English like your humble scribe and translator.

Without commentary or ornament, with only slight editing, I have loyally tried to record the voice I heard coming from below. Fatally, my poor language in English no more matches the Rock's eloquent French than did the pedestrian Latin of Aulus Gellius ascend to the soaring Greek of Favorinus. I sat on that spot, high on the hill, nearly at the top of the Rock of Arles, in the quartier of the city still called by an old, strange term, L'Hauture (or L'Auture), the Heights. From up there, the Rock of Arles has seen everything, and its memory is adamantine. It tells a stony tale, full of ups and downs—an auto-orography, if you like: a lapidarian mountain memoir.

The Rock *of* Arles

I

Urbs Dupleix

JE SUIS LE ROCHER D'ARLES, ET VOICI MON HISTOIRE. Whenever anyone speaks of Arles, they must inevitably mention me, the Rock on whom the city first arose. I am anomalous, a limestone eminence rising abruptly above the flatness all around, washed up by epochal waves clashing over millions of years—at a place where the violent Mediterranean Sea meets a furious Rhône River. My geology is long, but my history runs for only a few thousand years. Believe me, it's long enough—so ripe with beauty and drowned in blood that I'm forced to elide many luminous miracles and to omit innumerable disasters that have befallen those who, since the dawn of human time, have crawled over my shoulders. For the moment, I'll not even mention geological time, although at bottom it's my geology that tells me who I am. Sand and shells: I was once covered by inland seas. Sedimentation, not eruption, erected me here close by the mighty Rhône. Further north, at Lyon, the river is swelled by the Saône, its largest tributary, and from there it rushes south unimpeded through its great valley between the Alps and the Massif Central until it slams into my rock and abruptly veers west before continuing south to its mouth and emptying into the sea. I'll spare you most of all that, although it has its own alluvial fascination.

The patina blush at dusk that haloes buildings in Arles, on streets barely lit by the occasional lamp, emerges from deep within me. For I am the Rock, where enduring memory is lodged. I am immovable, listening to every whis-

I.1. Flowered Rock of Arles

per, but also farseeing, knowing many things from great distances away, told to me by rumormongering winds and gossipy birds. For centuries, since before Caesar, rock has been the sublime stuff on which cities have been founded: it lends them intimations of immortality. It tells the world that this city is eternal, so far as humans can imagine.

But nothing is eternal (except eternity). Not even the Rock of Arles. The city of Corinth erected a bronze statue next to the library to honor the genius of Favorinus. When he lost the favor of the emperor, the statue disappeared. As Favorinus used to say, "Of course I know that statues are erected to be eternal—are offered in perpetuity—but I also know that each thing perishes according to its destiny, the most common and the most just. It's the law of time."[1]

Officially, I rise thirty meters above the flat ground that lies all around, spreads out, and runs down to the Rhône. Geologically speaking, I am incongruous because of the way that I emerge so abruptly next to the river between a vast plateau on one side, called La Crau—more like a rocky steppe, on which, for centuries, only sheep could thrive on its stony soil—and, on the other, the Camargue, the marshy delta of the Rhône, where pink flamingos totter, where wild Arab horses and combat bulls excite the gypsy spirits that make Arlesians dream. I am also a natural redoubt and a lookout tower. Once the Romans arrived, I was girded by Augustus with great stone walls and flying arches. They served more to affirm the permanence and dignity of Roman conquest than to protect me. I have been invaded, set on fire, and occupied by many races, but I persist untroubled, waiting for a more perfect time. I am indurate.

At this delicate moment in the history of Arles, when it stands at a dangerous intersection, the city needs a vision of itself, to be reminded of its glorious imperial and revolutionary past, if it has any chance to escape the fate of other cities in Provence that have become museums, lost to the intensity of new beauty and fresh blood. Recently, Arles has been very poor; in the second century it was the capital of Gaul, the center of Roman power in all of Europe beyond the Alps. Arles has lately been a sleepy provincial town; in 1793 blood ran in the streets.

The limestone rock of which I consist is easy to excavate but renitent, extremely hard to crush. Conchiferous stone made up of shells and sand that once lay at the bottom of seas that covered Provence was compacted and slowly lithified into a single solid mountain by the endless cementation of an infinite plurality of grains. The limestone quarries out of which the oldest houses in Arles were drawn still exist in nearby Fontvieille, now greatly diminished but still surviving their limestone's replacement in recent times by reinforced concrete.

I.2. The limestone Rock of Arles

Down the road where they used to fix trains, in the old Parc des Ateliers, the rugged steel tower with its glassy skirt, built by Frank Gehry for the LUMA Foundation, intends, perhaps, to mirror me—a reflection of the original Rock of Arles that stabs the sky. The question must be asked: Does the skirted stainless tower reflect me, the Rock of Arles, or is it a new incarnation of that other erection at my foot, the high-towered Church of Saint-Trophime? I've had Christians on me for fifteen hundred years. They built their first cathedral on top of me, contemptuously using Roman stones. Then came convents and more churches. They are mostly gone now. I've watched the Church dissolve under the weight of its corruption and irrelevance. Notre-Dame is burning. The archbishop of Arles, once the most powerful churchman in all of Europe, outside the pope, is reduced to saying Mass for Boy Scouts, preparing catechumen for confirmation, while real estate brokers swarm to buy up old chapels for dance parties and redundant churches exhibit photos of artistic nudes.

The first mayor of Arles, Pierre-Antoine Antonelle, saw the future clearly in 1789, on the eve of the French Revolution, after fifteen hundred years of Christian clerics dominating life in Arles: "Morality is the work of feeling and reason. Religion is the dream of the imagination. One is true, the other chimerical. One is useful, and necessary, and beneficent, the other always superfluous and often harmful. One brings people together, the other divides them. One makes citizens, the other worshippers [*dévôts*]. One makes friends, relatives, spouses, and fathers, the other makes monks, priests, and nuns. One peoples the earth. And makes it fertile. The other makes it a desert."[2]

On his deathbed, Antonelle refused the sacraments and loudly cursed God and the Church.

For fifteen hundred years, Arles was known as a hidebound center of submissive piety, in thrall to the pope, oppressed by a conservative provincial nobility that ruled alongside a bigoted, authoritarian church. But the beating pagan heart of Arles will not be stilled.

The city must not be allowed to forget the revolutionary lessons of its greatest minds, the deep current of dissident humanism before it vanishes forever beneath waves of reaction, obscurantism, and inveterate superstition. Especially now when it faces a crossroad, the memory of its pagan heritage needs to be resurrected and evangelized before its transformative energy is lost forever.

You probably wonder why I've chosen you to be an instrument of the city's pagan revival, to bring the good news of an older Arles in view of its miraculous rebirth. I could hardly believe my luck when you bought your house on top of me. Of all the people who have lived here for centuries, there are

I.3. The Frank Gehry tower built for LUMA

few—very few—who have the sympathies required to tell the story of that other Arles. I know you've written with special regard for the intersexed, the blasphemers, and for revolutionaries. And being foreign you likely have a less biased, less conventional notion of the city's history. Your French is good enough that I can perhaps even assume that you appreciate the beauty of my language. If this auto-orography is ever rendered back into French, I can count on you to find a brilliant translator.

You can imagine that I felt moved by the unexpected honor, the burden of responsibility to transmit the words of the Rock as faithfully and eloquently as I could. I wondered too about what it would look like eventually to translate my English translation of the Rock's French back into a French translation of my English translation of the Rock's French. After a weighty pause, the Rock of Arles continued:

At least once in fifteen hundred years, in 1235, the plutocrats, nobles, and rich bourgeois rebelled against the autocratic, feudal power of the archbishop, and twice they chased him out of town. *La confrérie*, as they called themselves, were resolutely anticlerical. In 1235 they seized the archbishop's residence and pillaged it after having expelled the bishop, the hapless, vicious Jean Bausson. He was accused by Sirvantes de Bertrand de Lamanon of having assassinated Guilhem de Jonquières, a salt farmer, for no other reason than the desire to seize his fortune, although no one else ever found him at fault. The confrérie chased off the monks and seized their goods and cattle.

Several families found this to be an occasion to enrich themselves. Pons Gaillard took the bishop's cattle to his stable and kept them. Religious ceremonies were forbidden. People were fined a hundred sous if they paid the least sum to the clergy—if they brought offerings or did any work for the ecclesiastics or rendered the slightest service. The life of priests became difficult. Some bakers who had provided them bread were severely punished with fines. One of the members of the confrérie broke his cane over the head of a parishioner who had taken his child to the Church of Saint-Julien to be baptized. Bishop Bausson, who had taken refuge nearby in Salon, did nothing but issue excommunications and interdictions. The confrérie were not moved by them. Lamanon writes: "I take no account of his interdictions because a man who has been interdicted can't interdict me." Priests stopped marrying couples because of the interdictions. Pons Gaillard took his wife from the hands of a layperson through a simple civil contract. Arles had become a revolutionary, secular commune, violently anticlerical, led by plutocrats—the recently knighted and the rich bourgeois.

The anticlerical violence of the confrérie seems evidently to have been influenced by the Cathar heresy raging all around, to judge from certain symbolic actions such as the hostility to the Mass and the refusal of the sacraments of baptism and marriage.

In their hearts, after more than a millennium of rule by the Church, Arlesians have never forgotten the long-suppressed lesson taught by Favorinus, little celebrated, now forgotten, but once their favorite son. He used to say, "And life doesn't seem to me any different than a carnival parade: that's the lesson of our changing fortune," of our *metabolei*. Neither the anticlerical upheavals of the revolutions nor the Church's demise would have surprised him. He also said: "In time, anything that can happen will happen."

Antonelle, Favorinus, you've certainly never heard of them. But to me, and I knew them well, they were the greatest minds that Arles has ever produced, and the most radical. I should add one more name, even less celebrated, more subversive (defying millennia of Hebrew patriarchy), the brilliant poet and translator Ḳalonymus ben Ḳalonymus. His name in Greek, Kalos Nomos, with a Latin ending, is likely a Hellenization of *shem tov* ("good name") in Hebrew—the highest of spiritual crowns.

Favorinus, Ḳalonymus, Antonelle, all three were born in Arles, separated by thousands of years of its vast history—all three giants, dissident heroes in their own way of universal humanism, gender freedom, and representative democracy. Yet they have mostly disappeared into what we in French call the *oubliettes* of history. An oubliette, in case you don't remember, is a secret dungeon with a hole in the ceiling, usually in a castle, where people are thrown to be forgotten.

We have no images of Favorinus and none of Ḳalonymus; the only one we have of Antonelle is a hostile cartoon featuring a parade of Jacobins, where he is represented with the head of a wild boar. No other depiction has been found.

In recent times, each of these forgotten heroes has warranted being called *une Arlésienne au masculin*. The first Arlésienne is the central character in a story by Alphonse Daudet (once a neighbor of mine here in Provence)—a character who interacts with other characters but is never actually seen or heard, never appears in the story "in flesh and blood," as it were. The hero of Daudet's story falls hopelessly in love with a lady from Arles. He is about to marry her when he discovers her infidelity and kills himself. Since antiquity, Arlesian women have been said to be loose and easy, fickle and faithless, but irresistible. Her importance in Daudet's story has, rather, to do with her invisibility. We never "see" her, only hear about her, but she is on everybody's mind. Beckett's Godot is his Arlésienne; Favorinus, Kalonymus, and Antonelle are mine.

Funny thing [*drôle de chose*]: despite furious digging for more than a century, archaeologists have finally recognized that there are no prehistoric, Neolithic artifacts to be found on my sides, except for one—a single silex blade that was discovered, it shouldn't surprise you, by my most faithful servant and most attentive lover, the great historian and archaeological genius, the late Jean-Maurice Rouquette. It's said this absence of relics is mysterious, for all around the hills are full of dateless remains, tons of bits of prehistoric huts, and caves. But to me, of course, it's no mystery. I did not have any human settlements much before the fifth century [BCE]. Some Greeks from Marseille, some Ligurians from Italy, and finally the Celts built their huts on me until the Romans arrived.

For thousands of years, no one dared live on top of me. The single sharpened blade found by Jean-Maurice belonged to one fearless priest who had made bold to build his hut up here. He didn't stay long. With icy precision the mistral wind, blowing down the Rhône in February, blasted his hovel exposed on my rock until he had had enough, packed up, and left me alone untrammeled.

Around the globe we mountains have always been deemed to be sacred, have appeared awesome, even terrifying to those who lived at our foot. My sister Uluru, a great red sandstone rock in the middle of Australia, is still holy to the aboriginal Anangu, who, to this day, come upon it to worship and commune with Dreamtime, when the world was new. My mother, Gaia, belonged to the family of the Ourea, the primordial mountain gods. The early Greeks in Arles called me Oreios, assuming my prominence to be male. The Celts, who were on me when the Romans arrived, called me Caiiarus; but you can call me Pierre—or Petra, if you prefer. I've been taken for a great breast. They once called me and my city Mammilaria.

Like all those who came before, the Celts knew that I, like mountains everywhere, have this life, full of dreams, hopes, and despair. My sisters often explode with volcanic fury or sink into beclouded obscurity, leveled by roads or bored by tunnels. It is not easy to have seen and heard so much and to have forgotten nothing. Because I remember everything, I can foresee what's likely to come next. Imagine the rage, knowing at any moment exactly what must be done to forestall disaster or seize the chance but to be unable to do anything at all, to make the slightest move. Humans think that gods move the world when all we do is observe the carnival parade, rarely moved by it.

Like all gods, the Rock of Arles grows old and grows weary, beaten down, leveled off. But life on me has lately become more interesting, more fragile— as the world becomes more dangerous. Rocks ordinarily have little feeling for danger, for we are all but invulnerable. Because little frightens us, we are thrilled by the idea of something ahead, coming from the future: *l'a-venir*. We rocks have a nostalgia for the future from being so oppressed by the past. The accumulation of memories we can never dispel crushes us with their burdens in every waking moment. (You didn't think that mountains sleep?)

At this perilous time, the future of Arles, and perhaps that of the world, are deeply tied to memories of Favorinus, Ḳalonymus, and Antonelle, my mostly forgotten, queer, favorite sons. Queer—they were all three, in the usual meaning of the word in English, a little strange and peculiar in their social behavior, but they were also, in the American sense, recently adopted by the French, graced with perverse sexual and gender identities. It's their queerness that reflects a quintessentially Arlesian doubleness, riven with contradictions, the unstable foundation of their genius and their heroic imagination.

For almost two thousand years the liberating message of Favorinus has been obscured. It is an immense scandal that nothing remains in the city to mark the size of his achievement or even his passage, except for a tiny little twisted street, *la rue Favorin*, off the main drag [*la rue principale*], behind the restaurants on the Place du Forum, full of garbage overflowing and the clattering of pots and pans in the kitchens open to the street. Yet among all the children that have climbed on my sides, I have a few favorites, even favorite favorites, but none more favored than Favorinus, the personification of the genius of Arles: for, like Arles, he was profoundly double.

When the Romans conquered the city, they adopted its Celtic name and called it Arelate. They considered it an *urbs dupleix*, being cut in half by the Rhône, which divides the city center on the left from its other half, Trinquetaille, on the right, as you look down the river toward the sea. Separated from the center by 150 meters of the Rhône, Trinquetaille is not exactly a suburb, cut off as it is, but is considered part of Arles proper. For centuries the two halves were ruled by different counts.

How Trinquetaille got its name in the eleventh century is a mystery. The most poetic explanation was proposed by Mistral. He hears in *Trenquatalis* (the earliest form) two Provençal imperatives: *trenco* and *tailo*, meaning that

I.4. Garbage jam in the rue Favorin

the Rhône *tranche et taille* ("cuts and shapes") its delta. The violent river as it approaches the sea runs over millennial sandbanks, splits into two branches, and slices into many rivulets that shape the triangle of the delta, the watery plain of la Camargue.

For centuries the two sides of the river were joined by a famous bridge of boats lashed together that flexed (*fléchit*) with the mighty current. Wide enough to allow oxcarts to pass, it sometimes had a great platform in the middle where people would make a market and dance at feria to the sound of pipes twittering over the roar of the rushing Rhône.

Arles has been the home of Roman emperors and captured slaves, pagan temples and Christian spires, bloody revolutionaries and powerful papists, ruled by Pétainists and lately Communists. Once very rich, long very poor, Arles could now be on the cusp of transformation into a place of world historical importance.

Since antiquity, Arles has been a city with two ports, one on the sea, where deep-keeled ships brought goods from all over the Mediterranean, the other on the river, where skillful boatmen navigated the delta in flat-bottom boats to bring goods up as far as Lyon and beyond.

It has two great Roman monuments, the theater built by Emperor Augustus and the great arena, built later, modeled on the Coliseum in Rome. The one was devoted to Venus, the other to the huntress Diana—one to beauty, the other to blood. Arles today is still torn between its celebration of Van Gogh, who painted the beauty of Arles, and its devotion to Juan Bautista, the city's greatest torero, killer of bulls, now the manager of the arena.

It has been said that there is no place where you find so perfect a combination of Latin rule and barbaric force as in the city of Arles—order and violence, beauty and blood.

(Like Favorinus, the Rock of Arles will never be afraid to open a parenthesis.) I can't conceal that I have always found the city's proprietary reverence for Van Gogh more than a little presumptuous. The man lived here altogether for four hundred and forty-four days. Despite having made more than one hundred great paintings and innumerable sketches and watercolors, he sold only one painting while he was in Arles. He was viewed with the suspicion attached to bohemian foreigners, was aggressively disliked, cruelly treated, and eventually expelled—this after the honorable citizens of Arles had sent a petition to the mayor demanding the removal of . . . the greatest painter of the nineteenth century:

> We the undersigned, residing in the city of Arles, place Lamartine, have the honor to inform you that the man called Vood (Vincent), landscape painter, Dutch subject, living in the aforementioned place, has shown for some time that he does not possess his full mental abilities, and that he is given to an excess of drink, after which he is found in a state of overexcitement such that he is no longer aware, neither in fact, nor in speech, and is very worrying for all residents of the quarter, and mainly for the women and children.
>
> In consequence, the undersigned have the honor to ask, in the name of the public security, that the so-called Vood be sent back to his family; or that the necessary formalities are completed in order to admit him into an asylum, so as to avoid the misfortune that will certainly come one day soon if we do not take active measures in this regard.[3]

The mayor of Arles took active measures in this regard and shipped Van Gogh off to the asylum in St.-Rémy.

Androgynous, profoundly double, Favorinus was himself a living paradox who above all loved paradoxes. He once described himself, in the third person, with three seemingly irreconcilable contradictions:

A Celt, born in Arles, he was a great Hellenist;
a eunuch, he was prosecuted for adultery;
he quarreled with the emperor and lived.[4]

Favorinus was born in Arles at the end of the first century, at a moment when Rome was reaching the heights of imperial power. Emperor Titus had just conquered Jerusalem, and Rome was rich with spoils he had brought back from the Holy Land. On the walls of his arch, next to the Coliseum, I'm told you can still see pictured there his triumphal parade in Rome, led by the giant seven-branched candelabrum, the menorah, taken from the Temple in Jerusalem. To this day, religious Jews avoid the Arch of Titus.

Favorinus came from a family of comfortable, literate Celts who worked for the Romans in Arelate and lived in a big stone house at my foot, well below the houses of the Roman nobles, with Italian names, higher up. His family were local aristocrats who had changed their Celtic name to its equivalent in one that sounded Hellene. They had wealth enough to send their queer son to the best schools in Marseille and Rome. Favorinus had a sister he adored. With her he used to skip up and down my streets, playing with other Celtic kids and running from the jeers of little Roman bullies.

The Celts, you remember, were a tribe in Central Europe that spread their language and culture across Gallia for a thousand years until Caesar conquered them, smashed them, in 50 BCE — that's a date to remember. Roman control lasted five centuries, until the last so-called emperor, Romulus Augustus, was deposed. His barbarian enemies mocked him, calling him Augustulus (Little Augustus), or Momyllus, "little piece of shit." After him, in the fifth century, the Frankish barbarian Clovis ruled over most of what was once the Roman province of Gallia. With amazing speed, within a century or two, Gallic Celts had lost their language and their national identity and had melted into a Gallo-Roman culture that reflected its double origins: fierce Latin discipline and haughty Celtic pride. Gallia remained the conventional name of the territory throughout the early Middle Ages, before it was wrenched into the kingdom of France.

Despite having been settled for centuries largely by Celts and Ligurians from northern Italy, I was also inhabited briefly (two or three hundred years: the time it takes me to blink) by crafty Greeks [*in 600 BCE*] who had come here from Marseille (formerly Massalia) to set up shop on the Rhône and do business up and down the river. The Greeks had fled their native Phocea, on the Aegean coast, when their city was conquered by the Persians. Rather than submit to Persian rule, they abandoned the city and, great sailors, bravely navigated around the boot of Italy, landing near the mouth of the Rhône in the natural harbor of Marseille. There they founded a Greek colony that lasted several hundred years until the indigenous Celts pushed back and retook the city and its surroundings. During the Roman Empire, Massalia was, next to Athens, the greatest center of the study of Greek language and thought.

Legend has it that when Protis, the chief of the Greek sailors, arrived in Arelate from Massalia, it was by chance the very day the king of Arles, Nunna, leader of the tribe of Servobrige (which inhabited the Rhône delta), was arranging to marry his daughter, Gyptis, to whomever the princess chose to offer a cup of wine or water, as was the custom. All the Gallic princes were assembled with their hopes. The Greeks, having come on business, were invited by the king to attend the ceremony. Gyptis took one look at the Greeks and, without hesitation, offered water to Protis, so the foreign guest became the son-in-law of the barbarian king. The myth of the marriage of Protis, the Greek leader, with Gyptis, daughter of the Celtic king, symbolized the alliance of two peoples, in which the foreigner was fused with the native. It illustrates, as well, the desire of the Phocean Greeks from the beginning to appropriate the identity of the indigenous people or, conversely, to lead them to become Hellenized. Recourse to mixed marriages seems to have been necessary and widespread in the earliest periods of colonization. Most of all, perhaps, the myth confirms the seductive power and fierce determination of Arlesian women, who know what they want and how to get it. At the corrida, they are the first to arrive and the last to leave the arena, which echoes with the vehemence of their passionate aficion. As we say of Arlésiennes, "*Elles ont du caractère.*" [*Hard to translate: "They have attitude"?*]

By the time that Favorinus left the schools the Greeks had founded here in Arles, he was already perfectly fluent in three languages: Celtic, Greek, and Latin. To the amazement of his teachers, he began to orate magnificently, confounding those who had never imagined that a barbarian Celt could acquire such eloquence—particularly in Greek. He left Arles, they always do, to go to Marseille, the most important center of Greek life in the early Roman Empire outside of Athens, which by the second century [CE] had become a university town. It was said that Marseille combined the best of Greek politeness with the most charming provincial simplicity. "The study of Greek literature and philosophy," said Favorinus, "has been the principal, almost constant occupation of my life. However, I am not so little familiar with the Latin language—although I studied it only in my leisure and intermittently." In fact, as with Greek, he had read everything in Latin and had memorized most of it, enough to debate with the greatest Roman grammarians, and even—at his peril—with the emperor himself, over the smallest detail of Latin etymology.

For instance, in second-century Rome, among the so-called Sophists, there arose the etymological question: Does the Latin word *parcus*, meaning "frugal," come from *par arcae*, "like a strongbox"—that is, keeping everything close and guarded? Or rather, as Favorinus seems to know, with the authority of his vast erudition, does the word *parcus* actually come from *parum*, which means "too little, not enough"? Of course, sometimes, I'm afraid, even Favorinus gets it wrong. I happen to know, with adamantine certainty, that the Latin *parcus* is in fact related to *parco*, meaning "spare." Favorinus was merely able to quote from memory the entire works of Cicero. The Rock of Arles, a god, forgets nothing. However, Favorinus was also convinced, with some authority, that Greek was more beautiful than Latin.

Arles had already produced one famous Greek orator, Clodius Quirinalis, no Celt, who some say was a very great man of letters. He was born in Arelate, like Favorinus, and like him he studied in Marseille before becoming famous as a teacher of rhetoric and belles lettres. He was caught embezzling money from the emperor, and it was suggested that he commit suicide.

Martial mocked him in an epigram:

> Quirinalis doesn't think he should have a wife, though he wants to
>   have sons.
> He has found a way to achieve this: he fucks his slave girls [*futuit
>   ancillas*]
> and fills his town house and country estate with home-born knights
>   [*his bastards*].
> Quirinalis is a true *pater familias*.[5]

But *familia*, you know, sometimes means "slave establishment."

Quirinalis never attained the fame and notoriety of Favorinus, who was considered by many in the second century to be its greatest rhetorician and philosopher. I once heard him orate in Arles in the forum at my foot. He stood on the steps of the great temple of Augustus and spoke so sweetly that doves swept down like a cloud above his head. People wept to hear him praise the skies while speaking of meteorology. Even those who knew no Greek would come to marvel at the rhythms of his speech and the musicality of his intonations, and to observe the elegance of his gestures.

Favorinus grew up to be the Roman Empire's most cultured man, its greatest polymath. He was consulted by famous jurists for his knowledge of ancient Roman law; he advised doctors at the bedside of his friends with his vast knowledge of medicine and physiology. He was a man profoundly versed in all the domains of knowledge. He declaimed on and wrote about innumerable topics; along with Plutarch, he was the most prolific writer of his age. He was, as the Greeks called him, *aner polumathis kata pasan paideian*, a polymathic man who had cultivated everything that could be studied. Favorinus often spoke of his ambition to acquire all human knowledge, which in the second century might have seemed possible. His memory was extraordinary, called by some divine. He could spontaneously recite nearly the entirety of Greek literature. He worked incessantly, with tireless enthusiasm for study. He wielded his learning, which was disciplined and serious, combined with his immense rhetorical powers, as weapons in their power to persuade. He attracted the most brilliant disciples in Greece and Rome. Statues were erected in his honor in Athens and Corinth, and his name was widely heard throughout the empire in the same breath as that of Emperor Hadrian, with whom he was intimate—for a while.

In the Roman Empire, in the second century, it wasn't a good idea to talk politics in public. It could get you killed. At the same time, people, lacking other distractions, adored being entertained by great oratory. So the people they called Sophists, who went around from city to city declaiming to great acclaim, never spoke against power—unlike their fifth-century [BCE] namesakes. Think of Socrates, whose views condemned him to death for corrupting the youth. Second-century [CE] Sophists had one central theme: literature, which comprised all the forms of elevated language—myths, histories, dramas, fictions. Despite the general enthusiasm for rhetoric, the Roman orators of the second century produced no great works themselves, although, perhaps, never was the literature of preceding generations better appreciated and more closely studied.

An amiable and generous debater, Favorinus didn't rage and storm with indignation like other orators. He was all subtlety and wit and devastatingly accurate taunts and jibes directed at his enemies, of whom he had many. Hadrian was amused by his hypochondria; he said that Favorinus treated the health of his body as if it were a beloved mistress. As for his actual mistresses, he was constantly paying fines for adultery. Hadrian complained about regularly having to get him out of difficulties created by his immense libido and hordes of admirers in the provinces. Particularly in Arles, already famous in antiquity for the beauty of its women.

He had only one glaring defect in the eyes of the Romans. Not having been castrated, he was nevertheless what they called a eunuch, a term that covered a whole range of conditions. His—a kind of pseudo-hermaphroditism, known today as Reifenstein syndrome—resulted from undescended testicles; it permitted sexual activity, leaving him potent but sterile. It's called cryptorchidism—literally, "hidden orchids," that is, balls. It's the same word in Greek, *orchis* (to them, orchids looked like testicles; don't ask). The condition was said by his contemporaries to provoke "immoderate reproductive libido." In other words, he was very sexy and always horny (*lubrique*). The Romans generally took such physical aberrations, such sexual hybrids, to be monstrous—nature's sign of some profound moral depravity, unlucky to look upon. These people were dissolute, libidinous, unclean, unsuitable for doing philosophy, to be excluded from assemblies and shrines.

As with just about every aspect of Favorinus, there are two views of him: the view of his friends, who adored him, and the other of his enemies, whom he enraged. One of the most violent, his rival Polemon, described him as having a large forehead and flabby cheeks, puffed-up eyes, a wide mouth, and oily skin. His neck, writes Polemon, was long and thin "like that of a woman," but he had thick ankles and much flesh on the legs. His hair was perfumed; he wore makeup and took exaggerated care of his body. Favorinus was distinctly effeminate; his rivals called him a slutty queen (*cinaedus*). Yet angry husbands of high rank were constantly charging him with adultery. He would escape punishment by pleading his effeminacy. "How could a eunuch, who looks like me, with no beard, with a high-pitched voice and the gestures of a lady, be guilty of seducing such noble-born women?" he would ask the court indignantly. It never failed.

In the second century you could hardly claim to be a philosopher without possessing one essential attribute: a long, flowing beard. Seriously! It was an absolute precondition. Favorinus was beardless. He suffered his whole life from the discredit attached to this condition. Intersexuals were seen as abject instruments of infamous pleasure. In response to the ridicule that attended his claim to being a philosopher, though beardless, he would retort: "If it is by length of beard that philosophers are to be judged, a Billy goat would with greater justice be given preference to all of them!"

In Greek (and Latin), the notion of *eunuchos* comprised a great many conditions, most resulting from castration. It went from the total removal of the genitals to the mere cutting of the testicles. Depending on their age and the extent of the operation, some men were left with no libido and no sexual activity while others had full potency and were sexually active, with both sexes, top and bottom. The castrated priests of Cybele were notorious for their lascivious sexual activity.

Giving sexual pleasure, rather than receiving it, was considered unmasculine; eunuchs had no masculine reputation to uphold, so they provided women with forms of pleasure otherwise unavailable. Even those who were impotent had other means to give pleasure. Dildos were widely available.

Eunuchs in Rome were wildly attractive to women, particularly upperclass women who had probably been installed by their fathers in an arranged marriage with some prominent middle-aged ogre. They could dawdle with eunuchs with no fear of pregnancy, for which the consequences would have been disastrous.

There's another naughty epigram by the poet Martial:

Cur tantum eunuchos habeat tua Caelia quaeritis, Pannyche? Futui vel ut Caelia nec parere. (You ask, Pannyche, why your Caelia consorts with so many eunuchs. Caelia would rather be fucked than give birth.)[6]

Favorinus was not technically a eunuch, although throughout his life he was treated as one. His erotic career was undoubtedly enhanced by his having a condition that left him looking effeminate, fully potent but sterile. Eunuchs have been objects of desire in many cultures, seeming to offer the best of both worlds. They are often very sexy and very highly sexed, which made them promiscuous and shunned by the Roman system of values.

At the same time, eunuchs have occupied positions of power in many cultures, operating often brilliantly as diplomats and government officials, even famous generals. I've heard it said that generals in the army have been shown to have less testosterone than foot soldiers—corrected for age. It seems to suggest that less testosterone permits more strategic thinking, less spontaneous aggression, and greater foresight. This may explain why eunuchs have often been chosen as educators, managers, and administrators. Being liminal in their gender between male and female, they often served as go-betweens, crucial mediators in government and business; they were often entrusted with management of money, like that eunuch in the Gospels [*Acts 8:27*] of great authority under Candace, queen of the Ethiopians, "who had charge of all her treasure." They also had a universal reputation for loyalty and trustworthiness. In Medina, in 1990, seventeen eunuchs were the sole guardians of the prophet's tomb, as they had been since the twelfth century. Their trustworthiness recommended them to emperors in China who admitted them into their inner sanctums and relied on them as tutors to their children and as administrators of the state.

To his friends, Favorinus had a pleasant face and a gracious manner; he was able to correct his voice to make it pleasing and harmonious. Crowds in Rome gathered to hear him, charmed by his fluency and the graceful expressions of his features, even if the audience didn't understand Greek. Aulu-Gelle, his disciple, followed him around Rome as if chained to his lips, so besotted was he by what he called "the infinite grace of his discourse." He wrote: "We were almost every day in Rome with Favorinus—this man of such sweet eloquence had seized hold of our mind and wherever he went we followed, as if captivated by his words, such did he charm us in all circumstances with his agreeable conversation."[7] The principal characteristics of his eloquence were prolixity, charm, elegance, and exquisite grace of language. He was the sweetest man to hear: *dulcissimus* ("extremely sweet"); his oratory was also famously abundant, loquacious, you might say. One of his enemies said, "Yes, he is in every way an old woman."

I wish you could have heard him, seen him. There's not a single portrait that has survived. And if an artist today tried to imagine how he looked, he couldn't begin to tell from the contradictory descriptions we have of him. If Arles were ever going to erect a statue of him in the rue Favorin, it should probably have to be faceless.

Reflecting perhaps on the faceless statue, the Rock grew silent. I tried to imagine what a faceless statue might look like. I was about to get up and leave, when suddenly the Rock began to speak:

It's not because we don't have any images of Favorinus that his statue would need to be faceless. There are many statues whose sculptor has never seen the subject's face. The sculptor is authorized, even required, to model features more beautiful or more expressive than life. With respect to Favorinus, it was rather that he didn't have "a" face. He was multi-faced (faceted?), with expressions and gestures that were perfectly calculated to reflect (or ironize) the words he was speaking. His oratory spoke with his body. His gestures had a fluidity, his words a musicality that no stone or metal statue could convey.

With that, the Rock paused, and I rushed upstairs.

II

Quid Obstat Fit in Via

After a feverish night trying to write down as much as my aging memory and careful notes would let me remember, I returned the next morning to the cellar and waited a long time before the Rock once more began to murmur:

Romans in the second century loved everything Greek. You know, of course, that they had conquered and occupied the Greek world after the Battle of Actium in 31 BCE, when Caesar's adopted son, Octavius, soon to become Emperor Augustus, defeated Cleopatra, queen of Egypt, and her lover, the Roman general Marc Antony. Later, Augustus conquered Alexandria, the last great Hellenic city to fall under Roman rule. It's fitting that Arles should be known as the city of Augustus, for it was he, after the assassination of Caesar, who built it.

The elites of Roman society, in the second century, out of reverence for the customs and art of the much older and greater Greek civilization, adopted their architectural styles and took over the pantheon of their gods, giving them Latin names. They studied the Greek language, its writers and philosophers, especially Plato and Aristotle, and they took from the ideas of ancient Greek thought models of science and culture. The Roman poet Horace rightly said, *Graecia capta ferum victorem cepit.* ("Captive Greece captured her rude conqueror.")

Unconcerned with politics, discussions of which could be considered dangerous by imperial authorities, the second-century Sophists concerned themselves with more abstract, philosophical questions, and treated problems of everyday life. They asked, for example: Is it correct to invite a friend to accompany you to a banquet to which the friend hasn't been invited? Or should you not trust dreams that come in autumn, when they are often false? If you lie and say you're lying, are you telling the truth, or not? Why is *A* the first letter of the alphabet? Sophists offered guidance and wisdom, and they came to dominate higher education.

They left their mark on many forms of literature and on the language of morality. Favorinus used to say, for example, "Abundant wealth gives birth in men to new needs; the richer one is the more one wants to become richer, and the best way not to be assailed by incessant desires is to diminish one's fortune, not increase it."[1] He recounted that a Boeotian once by chance discovered a treasure when he was already seventy years old. After lifting his leg, he let go a fart and continued on his way, thereby demonstrating that this treasure had no value. So it is that old age extinguishes the desire to possess a lot of money or to undertake much business.

Philosophy came to be regarded as distinct from sophistry, the latter being considered casuistic and rhetorical, a more practical than purely intellectual discipline. So, by the time of the Roman Empire, a sophist was simply a teacher of rhetoric and a popular public speaker. However, Favorinus was widely regarded, by others and by himself, as, above all, a philosopher. He wrote many purely philosophical works: on the philosophy of Homer, on Socrates and his conception of the art of love, on Plato and Aristotle, on the conduct of philosophers. Few of his works have survived.

The insemination of Greek and Greeks into Roman society led to a rebirth of Greek oratory and education among Roman elites in the first and second centuries. The Sophists aimed to revive a purer form of the old religion and to encourage the cults of the heroes and Homeric gods. Roman emperors such as Trajan and Hadrian admired and respected these intellectuals and sought their company. Most of them reverenced all things Greek. Nero visited Greece in 66 [*CE*] and performed at the ancient Olympic games, despite the rules against non-Greek participation. He was honored with a victory in every contest. Emperor Hadrian, you know, was a great lover of Greece. Like Favorinus, he visited Athens many times; it was probably there that they met. He is said to have especially admired the extraordinary erudition of Favorinus and the finesse of his eloquence. He is supposed to have preferred reading the works of Favorinus to those of classical authors.

The emperor was given to wearing Greek dress in place of the imperial Roman toga, and he served, even while emperor, as a chief magistrate, as an archon of Athens. He richly endowed the city with temples and art. The Arch of Hadrian, resembling a Roman triumphal arch, was built in Athens to celebrate his arrival and honor him for his beneficence to the city. There were two inscriptions on the arch, facing in opposite directions, naming both the demigod Theseus and Hadrian as founders of Athens.

Hadrian was a mixed bag (*tout un mélange*). To me, the Rock of Arles, he has always seemed, after Augustus, to be the greatest Roman emperor. He spent half of his reign traveling to every corner of the empire, which by that time extended from Egypt to Britain, from Spain to Germany to Persia. From time to time, he would take a detour to put down some trouble on the border, but the empire was mostly at peace and at the height of its political and cultural power. Hadrian was the first of five good emperors after the nightmares of Tiberius, Caligula, and Nero. The last of the best was Marcus Aurelius, who was both a good emperor and a great Stoic philosopher. You know his *Meditations*. We mountains have a favorite Aurelian aphorism: *Quid obstat fit in via.* ("What stands in the way becomes the way.")

Never hesitating to pause to digress, I'd add that Commodus, the son of Marcus Aurelius and later his successor, was the first child born of an emperor to reign. Since Augustus, the heirs were always adopted. Not Commodus. A disaster, he was certainly mad. He used to dress in lion skins, considered himself to be Hercules reincarnated, and would fight in the arena against animals and other gladiators. It gives plausibility to the widely believed rumor that Commodus was the offspring not of the Stoic emperor Aurelius but of an adulterous affair between the ill-reputed empress Faustina and a hunky gladiator.

Commodus sponsored the Plebeian Games, in which he shot wild animals with arrows and javelins every morning, and fought as a gladiator every afternoon, winning all the fights. He killed hundreds of wild beasts at a time (lions, bears, hyenas, wild bulls—even a rhinoceros provoked to rage) with spears and arrows shot from a walkway suspended above the floor of the arena. When he fought other gladiators, they were graciously provided with wooden weapons.

Toward the end, Commodus declared himself the new Romulus and ritually refounded Rome, renaming the city Colonia Commodiana. All the months of the year were renamed to correspond exactly with his (now twelve) names: Lucius, Aelius, Aurelius, Commodus, Augustus, Herculeus, Romanus, Exsuperato, Amazonius, Invictus, Felix, and Pius. The legions were renamed Commodianae, the fleet that imported grain from Egypt was termed Alexandria Commodiana Togata, the Senate was titled the Commodian Fortunate Senate, his palace and the Roman people themselves were Commodianus, and the day on which these reforms were decreed was to be called Dies Commodianus. Madmen believe that anything to which they attach their name becomes an extension, an expansion of themselves. But names are written to be erased. Who does Commodus remind you of?

At the end, Commodus was poisoned by Marcia, his mistress, "assuming the courage of a man," it was said. He vomited the poison and wouldn't die. Finally, she sent his slave Narcissus to strangle him.

At news of his death, the Senate restored the name of Rome.

The emperor Hadrian was driven by intellectual curiosity and aesthetic ambition to paint and sculpt. He composed music and wrote in prose and verse. He was particularly enamored of Greek literature and spent much time in Athens, where he took on Greek manners and dress. In his youth he was nicknamed Graeculus ("the little Greek"). Hadrian was jealous of rhetoricians, grammarians, and philosophers, to the point that he often deprived them of their functions and took away their public positions for no reason or for spurious ones. Even with his closest friends, he would pile them with riches and favors, then abruptly consider them his worst enemies and reduce them to poverty, to exile, and even to death. It was a way of demonstrating his sense of his own intellectual superiority and power to the intellectuals of the court, whom he would venerate and then despise.

Favorinus, for long a favorite of Hadrian, knew the difficult and authoritarian character of the man and had managed skillfully for a while to escape his anger until he was chosen by the emperor for the dubious honor of being one of his archpriests (an *archiereus*) back in Gallic Arles. The title designated the head of the temple hierarchy in a province or a city. An archpriest was charged with performing sacrifices in honor of the emperor, offering up prayers to him and his family, and guarding his temple. A high honor, it would take a lot of his time and incur plenty of expense. You needed to have a considerable fortune to serve an immensely prestigious but costly public function. Favorinus resisted. Though by then quite rich, he had very little reason or desire to abandon his ebullient cosmopolitan life in Rome to return to his provincial roots in Arles—however much he frankly assumed his Celtic identity. Hadrian was furious at his refusal to be elected, but he relented when reminded of the exception that was commonly made for philosophers, which Favorinus, even without having a beard, claimed with good reason to be.

Later, something else, probably trivial, pushed Hadrian's anger to the point of sending Favorinus into exile. To the emperor's perversity was added his fury at Favorinus for repeated adulteries, for his lascivious behavior. To that was doubtless added the malevolent influence of his rivals, who were fiercely critical of his person and his work and whose partisans provoked regular battles in the streets of Rome.

Maybe the dispute wasn't trivial at all. Favorinus, with his anti-imperial, democratic instincts, his hatred of tyranny, and his freethinking polytheism, may have refused Hadrian's honor because he despised the idea of becoming a high priest of the emperor's cult.

The emperor might normally have been expected to punish such an insulting refusal with death. Instead, Hadrian, out of some sympathy and admiration, condemned Favorinus to a soft exile on the island of Chios, famous in antiquity for its wine and pretty women. He was obliged to remain in exile until Hadrian finally died and, after the accession of Emperor Antonius Pius, could return to Rome, to his library, his household, and his friends. From this whole misadventure, he drew an infallible conclusion: "It's never wise to argue a point of philology with a man who has thirty legions."

In exile, Favorinus learned a magnificent lesson. To convey it, he wrote a little book in Greek, *Peri Phugeis* (*On Exile*). During five years in Chios, far from family, friends, and profession, he came to realize that there is in fact no such thing as exile. Only those can be exiled who, to begin with, think they have a native land, a *patrie* to which they have some eternal bond because they were born there, or their parents were born there, and hence they hope to die there, like a mouse in its hole. But humans are not like mice. They more closely resemble other animals, like birds or whales, who have no native land, who are at home wherever they decide to dwell or perch their nest and call it home. Birds and whales, like humans, are migrants, said Favorinus; they are constantly changing places. In fact, who can deny that, in the past, we all came from somewhere else—that all of us, once upon a time, were foreigners and exiles? Once we moved here, we shortly decided that the here and now was sacred. Patriotism is a myth propagated by humans not content to live like birds. Instead, the first thing they do is build walls:

> But men, out of greed [*cupidité*], divide up the earth by dividing the gift of divinity into different parts: they divide by rivers like those between Asia,

Europe, and Africa, by mountains dividing neighboring countries by walls between compatriots, by doors between members of the same family; and now humans even separate those who live in the same room by closets and drawers. From which follow wars, sieges, destruction of houses and pillage. Erecting these walls, humans act as if they were combatting a foreign country. However, a bird doesn't dispute with other birds for a part of the sky, nor a fish with another fish over a beach or a rock because he believes that wherever he happens to be is his native land.[2]

Favorinus celebrates navigation, movement, migration. He particularly admired the migrating spirit of the Phoceans, who founded a whole other civilization at Marseille and built great schools and libraries in the place where he himself, after leaving Arles, had acquired his mastery of Greek oratorical arts and philosophical argument.

It is this philosophy that allowed him to endure and, you might even say, enjoy his exile while on Chios. It wasn't too burdensome. Not only because he was rich and Chios full of charms. But, above all, because, as Favorinus would write, exile is a state of mind. Storks, he further observed, have a soul nobler than ours. They migrate from Egypt to Thrace, but they don't consider either Thrace or Egypt to be their country of exile; they merely pass from their summer residence to their winter one without lending it any sort of importance. Just because my parents lived in a place does not mean that I must live there too. I can move to another country and still feel proudly loyal to my native land. Anyway, it's more natural to love the country you're living in than the one your ancestors lived in—and the same is true for your descendants.

Of course, in exile you may miss your friends. But if they are really friends, says Favorinus, they will come to visit, and if they don't, they were never friends to begin with. Favorinus takes his model of friendship, like many other values, from the life of animals. Can there be better friends than larks, which always accompany humans wherever they live, or plovers, birds that feed on harmful parasites in the mouths of crocodiles? Despite belonging to different species, they can never be far from their friends. Favorinus find his models for human life between the behavior of animals and the actions of heroes and gods. He wasn't saying that to be happy in exile you should hate your native land. That would be impious. But you shouldn't give yourself unnecessary pain with useless suffering out of some immense nostalgia. It's better to make the memory of your native land a source of joy rather than suffering.

I deplore the way the memory of Favorinus has been neglected in Arles.

Like Kalonymus and Antonelle, his example provides a controversial, polemical view of the city, more heterodox than the one to be found, for example, in its semiofficial history titled *Arles: Histoire, territoires, cultures* (1,297 pages of very small print), voluminous, magnificent—written and edited by the genius of the Rock, as I was saying, my latest, greatest favorite son, Jean-Maurice Rouquette. Just before he died last year, past eighty, Jean-Maurice lived with difficulty, alongside his brilliant wife, herself a great scholar, up here on me, hard by the redoubt of Arles, up against the still-standing Roman walls made of beautifully fitted small stones, to which the city retreated in moments of last desperate defense against millennial invaders—Roman, Christian, Muslim, pirate, and barbarian of every stripe.

Here at the very height of L'Hauture, at the highest point of the top of me, the people of Arles used to come to celebrate the god and goddess who gave them hope for abundance, for freedom from want, and whose festivals allowed them to inflame their *ardent* sexual desires. By the sixth century, the bishops had effaced from their dioceses all trace of those festivals, but they could never finally erase the carnival of Mardi Gras or the ferias that punctuate the seasons for killing bulls.

Rouquette's house stands smack in the middle of the ecclesiastical compound that was first erected up here in the sixth century by St. Césaire, an archbishop with megalomaniacal ambitions. He wanted above all to commandeer the space that once was the command tower of the Romans, whose pagan legacy he was determined to eradicate—along with some Jews. He was himself an ascetic monk and remained one, even as he became the most powerful primate in Gaul by fending off the heretical tribes of barbarian wolves, Goths and Visigoths, that surrounded his flock and its churches. He spent much of his time, still in the sixth century, denouncing pagan practices and warning his flock against widespread forms of pagan superstition: "Rather than having recourse to prayer to achieve their wishes, the faithful have recourse to incantatory practices addressed to supernatural forces. These practices can take the form of disguises allowing someone to pass for another (an old woman) or for an animal (a stag). God has chosen the gender and nature of each human; the faithful therefore commit a sacrilege by not respecting his will."[3] No disguise, no theater, no metamorphosis, no Ovid . . . no transsexuals. Conversely, pagan culture lives in a world where at any moment a god might appear in an epiphany, in the person of an old woman. Or Acteon, at Diana's command, can be turned into a stag. Nothing is as it seems.

Césaire denounces as well those who, "like animals, go around howling when the moon is in decline," or address their wishes to the elements: "making wishes to fountains or trees." Césaire anathematized forms of divinatory practice exercised by those condemned "to burn where the devil burns"—persons he characterizes as "magicians," "soothsayers," "enchanters," "sorcerers," or even—and here the link with Greco-Roman religion is clear—"aruspices" (those who predict the future by observing natural phenomena such as lightning, earthquakes, or animal entrails and most likely worship Jupiter). Finally, Césaire condemns superstitions that hold to the belief that objects can protect, by having recourse to amulets or pieces of amber: "Those who allow themselves to be tempted by these diabolical practices risk no longer being permitted to receive the holy sacraments and finally being condemned to burn in Hell."

In his youth the saint had already written a book of rules governing monastic life, and later composed "Rule for Virgins," which became the model for the monastic life of women. Many rules he took directly from previous monastic prescriptions; others he adapted in order to regulate every aspect, even the most intimate, of women's lives. He had rules on hygiene and baths, on coiffure, on embroidery and wool work, on renouncing elegance. Once a woman entered the convent, she was not allowed to leave; she was enwalled behind a strict, perpetual enclosure where she was expected to live until she died. This imprisonment was thought necessary to protect women from the dangers and temptations of the world, from the corruption and frivolity that might distract them from their blessed vocation. In a letter to his newly recruited sisters, Césaire congratulates them for choosing to spend the rest of their lives behind his walls:

> You have mastered the fire of passions, and you have attained to the freshness of chastity.
>
> You have rejected gluttony and have chosen abstinence.
>
> You have repudiated avarice and lust, and you have guarded your chastity and your mercy.
>
> And, although, until the end of your life, you won't lack for struggles, with God's help we are sure of your victory.

Then after the praise comes the threat, quoting Paul: "Hear the Apostle Paul, who says: Be sober and vigilant because your adversary the Devil is prowling around you like a roaring lion looking to devour someone. As long as we live in this body, day and night, with the help and under the direction of Christ, let us resist the Devil."[4]

In 1942, a second ago, the archbishop of Arles organized a public-relations event intended to commemorate the life and teachings of Caesarius and to flatter the Nazi occupant, who, it was hoped, would take St. Césaire as a model for what a good Christian leader should do: ruling over his flock, upholding right doctrine, performing charity, displaying piety, denouncing Jews—what a Christian leader could accomplish in the midst of barbarians and wars.

It was the first time such a whole public-relations campaign was organized in Arles—press releases, radio broadcasts, celebrity appearances. All this was overseen by the archbishop of Arles, Florent-Michel-Marie-Joseph du Bois de la Villerabel [*1877–1951*], with the aim of rallying the church behind support for the cultural face of the Vichy regime. Regrettably for some, the archbishop's celebration fell on a day in August, the fourteenth centenary of Caesarius's death, when, bracketing it—the day before and the day after—there was a vast roundup of foreign-born Jews.

Despite the unpleasantness surrounding the occasion, bishops, under the direction of the Reverend du Bois de la Villerabel, assembled at the old monastery in Lerins and addressed a telegram to the chief of state, Maréchal Pétain, on September 19, 1942, the fourteenth centenary of he "who founded Christian France." Here I quote from memory a report of the day that appeared in *L'Echo d'Alger*, August 27, 1942.

> Monseigneur the archbishop of Arles, the archbishop of Aix, the bishops of Fréjus, Nice, Monaco, the Most Reverend Abbotts of Lérins, Frigolet, the clergy and faithful, assembled at Lérins to celebrate the XIVth centenary of Saint Césaire, monk of Lérins and bishop of Arles, who contributed to founding Christian France, address to the Head of State [Maréchal Pétain], the savior and reconstructor of the Fatherland [la Patrie], the respectful assurance of their loyal veneration [N.B.] and their entire collaboration [!] in his work of religious, moral, and material recovery [redressement!!] of the [God help us!!!] new France. The Maréchal thanks the clergy of the southeast for their expressions of fidelity.

L'Echo went on to report that after the bishops' address in Provençal to Madame Pétain and a walk to the sea, the party was escorted to the fortified church of Saintes-Maries-de-la-Mer, where Archbishop du Bois de la Villerabel asked Madame Pétain to relay the homages of the faithful gathered in the church "to the one who works so happily for the resurrection of the country." He then spoke of "imperishable France," its present sorrows, and its future, in which it was necessary to have faith. This was followed by the customary lowering of the reliquaries into the sanctuary and the close of the ceremony.

Only ruins remain of the compound where Césaire in the fifth and sixth centuries built his church and convent on the highest point of L'Hauture, close to God, surveying everything. Now there are only some odd chapels and parts of the once great convent, but for those of long memory and pious disposition, it reflects the history of the city's persistent, fierce piety, which for too long, if you ask me, has overlaid the still-beating pagan heart of Arles. The churches erected on that spot to replace the influence of pagan Rome now lie in broken ruins and scattered pieces next to the still-standing Roman walls.

A Rock, I remember one moment when Christian piety saved the city. Thirteenth-century crusader armies, at the pope's command, descended the Rhône on their way to eradicate the Cathar heresy from Provence. They skipped right by orthodox Arles, with its long history of powerful bishops and papal deference. Already in 1205, the papal legate, Pierre de Castlenau, presided over a synod in Arles that excluded from city councils and from all public functions heretics and anyone suspected of heresy. He was later assassinated, by a spear to the kidneys, while crossing the bridge to Trinquetaille on his way to excommunicate the Count of Toulouse, suspected of protecting Cathar heretics. His murder so shocked the pope, Innocent III, that he didn't speak for three days, then launched the crusade against the Cathars. The crusading barons from the North, followed by an army of rabble, bypassed Arles and went farther west, straight to Beziers; there they massacred the entire population—set them afire in the church of Mary Magdalene, where they had sought sanctuary. Only the Vicomte of Beziers escaped ahead of the crusaders; he took with him the whole population of Jews, knowing what they would face at the hands of the crusaders.

It was on that notorious occasion that the commanding archbishop, the bloody Arnaud Almaric, having been asked how to distinguish heretics from Christians, replied: "Kill them all. God will know his own." Shortly afterward, the consuls of Arles agreed to lend financial help to the crusaders, promised to deliver over to the army those suspected of heresy, and swore to obey the orders of the pope.

In the thirteenth century the Franciscan friars installed their convent across the river in Trinquetaille, on a vast tract of land given them by its owner, the Count of Baux. One day, as St. Anthony of Padua, the first disciple of St. Francis, was preaching to the assembled brothers in the chapter about the Cross, one of them, Father Arnold, ecstatic, turned toward the door and saw with his own eyes of flesh St. Francis himself, elevated in the air, arms outstretched to form a cross, blessing the assembly. Only St. Anthony and Father Arnold had the epiphany. The others, heads bowed, attended to the sermon. The miracle became famous for decades in literature and painting. Giotto in Assisi, I'm told, painted a magnificent *Apparition of St. Francis to the Chapter of Arles*.

Although I have a longer view, my story of Arles is much more concise than Rouquette's exhaustive history, which weighs in at twenty-seven pounds, making it all but impossible to hold and read. Mine will cover the same span of time in some hundred pages with large print. He assembled the greatest archaeologists and historians of Arles—of its art and culture, its geology and archaeology—and organized their reflections into a masterpiece of historical, scientific, and artistic description. Not only does Rouquette write history; he also makes it. Much of the archaeological digging, analysis, and reimagining, which makes the book so valuable, was done by Jean-Maurice himself, out there in the dirt and rock, digging, digging, uncovering the immense life of ancient Arles. One of the book's greatest admirers called it a "folly," as if Rouquette had been impelled by a kind of Favorinian ambition, as if he were trying to include in this enormous, unwieldy book everything interesting that could possibly be said about the city he loved—everything that might ever have happened of any importance in 2,600 years. I naturally like to think it's a monument to me, the Rock of Arles, to the city and its monuments still on my side. It may even outlast my imperturbable stones.

Nevertheless, what I'm about to tell you is quite another side of things—Arles from the perspective of an old rock. Inspired by Favorinus, Ḳalonymus, and Antonelle, it is also a contrarian history that looks with skepticism, not to say cynicism, at what has been officially seen as a great achievement, fifteen hundred years more or less of Church domination. The Catholic Church, as you know, has by now been fatally discredited worldwide, from Ireland to Australia to Philadelphia. No one can be allowed to believe anymore what its clergy says, when you think of the hundreds of thousands, maybe millions, of young boys and girls, mostly boys, who, over centuries, have been preyed on by lascivious priests and bishops around the world, chafing at their celibacy. It's an old story. In the eleventh century things got so bad up here that St. Peter Damian had to write to Pope Leo IX in 1049 to tell him to put a stop to priests preying on young boys while being protected by their bishops, who, even worse, sometimes joined in: "O Unheard of Infamy! O Crime that a whole fountain of tears should cry! If those [bishops] who consent to what others do deserve death, then what torture do they deserve who join in these extreme evils, insuring damnation with their spiritual sons? The sodomist superior not only makes a concubine of the novice he spiritually fathered, but he submits him like a slave to the iron tyranny of the devil."[5] Think of it. Nothing has changed in a thousand years of priests making choirboys their concubines, while bishops join in.

Just suppose for a moment that the miracles recounted in the Bible and in the Gospel never actually occurred. Suppose they were all, at worst, cynical priestly inventions, at best, wistful fictions prompted by self-delusion. Some might call them lies. Yet at the time of St. Augustine, even the greatest minds took miracles to be almost daily occurrences. In *The City of God*, Augustine recounts at least seventy in his diocese alone about which there can be no doubt, including three resurrections. Think then of the fact that for fifteen hundred years, the institutions founded to promote these lies, those delusions, governed the mental life of European civilization. In their name whole cities were christened, architectures devised, monuments erected, and millions submitted their lives to its rituals and beliefs, while its priests were sodomizing children.

Jean-Maurice Rouquette himself was deeply pious, a conservative, traditional Catholic, which explains in part why he lived among the remains of the old convent erected by St. Césaire, in the sixth century, on the heights of me, next to the Roman walls. It pained him deeply to reflect on the ruins all around him of the Church he loved deeply and that he deemed central to the idea of Arles, which he may have loved even more. For Jean-Maurice, Arles was a holy city.

The death of Jean-Maurice was widely mourned in Arles and beyond. The Rock of Arles would weep for him, too, if rocks had tears. Up there in Heaven, if there were such a thing, let him forgive the Rock for its blasphemy.

I would hate to pain him. But an old Rock sees everything and can only tell you the truth.

With that I understood that the session was over. I reflected on the Rock's loss. No rock had a better friend or a more loyal chronicler than Jean-Maurice Rouquette. His very name sounds like "little rock" in French ("Roc-ette").

Colonia Julia Paterna Arelate

The weather had cooled, but the next afternoon I took my place in the cellar and waited for a long while. Suddenly, the Rock of Arles began again to tell his story in what I took to be a more somber tone.

(I wrote "his story" thinking perhaps to make the pun, but nothing warrants assigning a gender to the Rock of Arles.)

I am always surprised that humans think they can understand a poem or a story only by proceeding from its first line to the last. This story has no beginning, middle, and still no end. You might mistake it for the picaresque novel of a peripatetic philosopher, wildly speculating, except that what it's telling you is all true, all of it, and the Rock is not walking around. It is lapideous, petrifactive, immovable, perdurable, intractable, adamantine, fixed in place once and for all until it dissolves, one day, under the waves of some future flood.

A Rock, I have only two aims: to celebrate the glory of Arles in the second century and to illuminate the divine tolerance of its greatest minds. The Rock is speaking on the chance that you will convey the glorious past of Arles to its future and transmit the mission of Favorinus, the dreams of Ḳalonymus, and the vision of Antonelle to the city and to the world that has forgotten their lessons and needs them more than ever.

So why not begin today, August 21, the beginning of Roman days in Arelate. Tonight, in the antique theater, perched on me, the Rock, they will show old

Hollywood gladiator films in order to remember in their way the fateful day in 46 [BCE] when Tiberius Claudius Nero (no relation to the later Nero, but father of the future emperor Tiberius), acting under instruction of the first consul, Julius Gaius Caesar, stood, perhaps on the very spot that later became the stage of the theater (more a temple altar than a proscenium), and placed the Celtic city of Arelate under Roman law; declared it to be a Roman colony, the first across the Alps (except for Narbonne, another story); and donated it to his Sixth Legion veterans. Caesar intended it to become a little Gallic Rome where veterans might peaceably retire after twenty years of bloody service under his command.

Once a year, even today, men dress up in Roman soldier gear, exactly like what was worn into battle by Caesar's legions. They march through the streets of Arles, a whole company of them under command, superb in leather, some in leopard skins, muscled and barely dressed, carrying long spears and short swords, heavy shields, and legion standards, while officers shout orders at them in Latin. They march down the rue Porte de Laure, under kitchen windows, where locals once watched long ago in terrified amazement and wonder.

The soldiers are usually followed by matrons and girls dressed in white flowing Roman robes, waving flowers, and accompanied by their men in tunics and togas, while people in the narrow streets of L'Hauture stand in their doorways. For me, the Rock of Arles, it's as if another world, like a palimpsest, were still intact under the present streets but hidden and now suddenly emerged, as if I the Rock were still in Roman Arles when the city came alive.

It wasn't a happy day in 46 BCE, when Victrix, the Sixth Legion of the Roman army, marched into town under a broiling Midi sun. You can imagine the feelings of the Celts who had been here for centuries, not to mention the Ligurians, originally from northern Italy, who had been here even longer. They grumbled, dreamed of revolt, but soon enough started to love the wealth and science and law the Romans brought in their wake. All Roman citizens were equal before the law. In 48, Emperor Claudius gave citizenship to Gallic nobles; eventually, Emperor Caracalla granted citizenship to nearly everyone, except slaves.

At first, the Romans placed the city under military occupation, not for the last time in history. Moorish Saracens profited from a local's betrayal and seized the city for a while in the so-called Dark Ages and turned the arena into a fortress. Terrible Catalans came down from the Pyrenees and sacked the city. During the revolution the army of Marseille took back the town and chased the royalists who had seized the city council. During the Occupation,

the German High Command bivouacked in the Hotel Nord Pinus and flirted with Arlésiennes. Each time we are invaded, people get on with their lives, and I take a longer view.

When the Greeks arrived, they called the city Théliné, about which there is some dispute. There are those who think it means "swampy," from the Greek *telme*. That's basically what Arles means, a word that comes from the Celtic *Arelate*, which means the place "near" (*are-*) "the marsh" (*-late*), marking the city's site at the head of the Camargue, the marshy delta of the Rhône, where pink flamingos, wild horses, and bloody mosquitoes breed. In antiquity the delta was riven with multiple little branches of the river as it spilled over sandbanks into the sea, making its navigation a high art in which the boatmen of Arles were renowned. Boatmen down by the Rhône had perfected their seamanship in flat-bottom boats that alone could pass the sandbars, sand and silt piled up at the delta over millennia. Their boatyards on the Rhône famously built twelve fighting ships in a month, a record time, to allow Caesar to defeat Pompey in the waters off Marseille. Some want you to believe it was out of gratitude that Caesar chose Arles to be his first colony.

There are those who hear in *Théliné* a word derived from the Greek *thélé*, which means "nipple" or "teat." Or, more politely, "that which nourishes." The Latin poet Avienus in the fourth century referred to that old name of Arles. He wrote: "There arose the city of Arles, named Théliné (the nourisher [*la nourricière*]) in preceding centuries when the Greeks inhabited it."[1] The Greeks meant to indicate the richness of its surrounding lands and pastures. Like the Nile, the Rhône overflows its bank each year, or used to, before dikes and drains managed the floods. The lands of the delta were higher than they are now, so consequently less salty. It made the watery Camargue, from which Arles derived its prosperity, as fertile as Egypt, the great breadbasket of the empire.

Just as the point of a pyramid is its whole point, I gain the widest perspective and authority from up here, L'Hauture, from where I dominate the vast landscape, still the largest commune in France, all of it given to Roman soldiers to support their colony. Even more than its river commerce, Arles has always depended for its prosperity on the products of its fertile land stretching from the ocean to the Alps.

From this height I see almost everything and forget practically nothing. Like a pyramid, my serene exterior hides vaults of memory filled with innumerable inscriptions and the chaotic sense of lives. In place of a rich inner life, I have banks full of memories and resounding voices that have echoed around my stones for almost three thousand years, a place of memory with myriad stories to tell.

But by calling it Teat, they could have been alluding to me, the Rock of Arles, who, rising up, departs so prominently, so beautifully from the flat land all around. Such a name for a mountain would not be surprising if you think of all the old volcanoes in Wyoming, voluptuously rounded, I'm told, called Grand Teton or Petit Teton. It's why some Romans translated the city's name from Greek to Latin and, for a while, called it not Théliné but Mamellaria. So if you need to think of me as having a gender, the rounded Rock of Arles is more a generous swelling than a jutting protuberance.

About 550 BCE, fifty years after the first Greeks settled in Marseille, over the dead bodies of indigenous Celts and Ligurians, they set up shop to the west, on the Rhône, in the city they called Théliné. Two hundred years later, the Celts pushed back hard and retook the city. Yet memories of Greece and Greek schools were still circulating in Arles well into the Middle Ages, and to this day the city preserves a cultivated taste and sophisticated enthusiasm for history, literature, and translation. The recent minister of culture has her bookstore and publishing house on the quay. A school of translation has its home here. Need I mention the time from the twelfth to the fourteenth century when Arles was a great center of secular Hebrew studies, translating ancient Greek and Arab texts on medicine, science, and philosophy—before it chased its Jews?

The city has kept its Roman name except for one moment in the fourth century, when Emperor Constantine I, the Great, who loved Arles and built a palace near the Rhône, lent his presence and for a time his name to the city he called Constantinia. Marinus, the evil archbishop of Arles, the most powerful priest in all of Gaul, was his mentor. About him I'll have more to say.

The palace built by Constantine next to the river was the theater of major events in the reign of the emperor: his marriage with Fausta, the birth of his son, Constantine II. It was here that his former ally Maximian attempted to seize Constantine's title while the emperor was on campaign on the Rhine. Few supported him, and he was captured by Constantine in Marseille, reproved for his crimes, and stripped of his title for the third and last time. Constantine granted Maximian some clemency but strongly encouraged his suicide. In July 310, Maximian hanged himself.

Constantine initially presented the suicide as an unfortunate family tragedy. By 311, however, he was spreading another version. According to this, after Constantine had pardoned him, Maximian planned to murder Constantine in his sleep. Fausta learned of the plot and warned Constantine, who put a eunuch in his own place in bed. Maximian was apprehended when he killed the eunuch. In addition to the propaganda, Constantine instituted a *damnatio memoriae* on Maximian, destroying all inscriptions referring to him and eliminating any public work bearing his image.

Centuries later, Arles was a jewel in the crown of the Holy Roman Empire beyond the Rhine. In 1178 the archbishop of Arles solemnly crowned the Holy Roman emperor Fréderic Barbarosa as king of Arles. He was accompanied here in great pomp by the empress and his youngest son, Philip. The ceremony was celebrated in the great Romanesque Church of Saint-Trophime in the center of Arles, in the presence of the whole episcopate, all the bishops of Provence, and a crowd of local lords and ladies. The whiff of imperial ambition—

the ghost of royal empire has always hovered over the ruins that I harbor on my sides.

It was about this time, in the twelfth or thirteenth century, when heraldry was being invented by the nobility, before spreading throughout the upper classes, the city of Arles adopted as its emblem the banal figure of the lion. Unlike the elegant English lion, the Arlesian lion is seated, not rampant, seen not in profile but turned full face toward the spectator, with a paw upraised, holding a labrum and with a quizzical simian expression. As if to confirm its identification, the city maintained a living lion until the sixteenth century. No one has found a firm explanation for why the city fathers chose a lion, the most widely used animal in heraldry. Some say it was to distinguish it from the eagle of the Holy Roman Empire. In its first incarnation the golden Arlesian lion was represented against a white or silver background, which violated a cardinal rule of heraldic representation: metal cannot appear next to metal. It was the heraldist of Louis XIV who decided to correct the grievous error and henceforth to endow the golden lion with an azure blue background, and these have remained the colors of Arles.

I still bear stones on which the Romans carved the name of the city as Arelate Sextanorum—Arles of the Sixth Roman legion. Caesar sent his trusted lieutenant Tiberius to install the occupation of the city by the Roman army, to survey it, and to distribute its lands to the soldiers. He declared Arles to be a *colonia*, lending it a "deduction," which meant its inhabitants, Roman as well as Celt and Ligurian, were now subject to Roman law, with its magistrates and nobles who ruled the municipal council like a sort of senate. By the time that Augustus had pacified the empire, there were a half a million veteran fighters looking to retire. They accomplished the colonization of Gaul.

Caesar was assassinated on the Ides of March, 44 BCE, a year or so after founding Arles. But his ghost has never left my precincts. His soldiers often engraved the initials C.I.P.A. on my walls and monuments. They stand for Colonia Julia Paterna Arelate; Julius Caesar, *paterna*, the father of the city, belonged to one of the oldest Roman families, the gens Julia. He adopted Octavius, who took the family name and was forever known as *filius*, the son, even when he changed his name from Octavian to Augustus, meaning "esteemed, venerable, grown great," from the verb *agere*, "to increase."

Caesar had founded the colony of Arles hot from his smashing victory over Vercingetorix. It was in the first century BCE that the Roman armies invaded Gaul and massacred the Celtic nation. Wantonly they pillaged and burned everything from Spain to Germany, from Italy to Wales. "Eight hundred cities

III.2. The Lion of Arles protecting the City

taken by force, three hundred tribes made to submit, a million of the enemy killed, another million reduced to slavery," according to Plutarch. The Roman peace, *Pax Romana*, lasted almost three hundred years, with no major conflicts. When was there ever a longer period of peace and relative tranquility? After so much bloodshed and cruelty?

Vercingetorix, raised by priestly druids, trained in combat, tall, blond, and looking gorgeous, gathered up the remnants of the Celtic tribes who refused to submit to Rome. He was duped by Caesar and scandalized by the cowardice and deceit of the other Gallic chiefs. But he fought ferociously for the liberation of Gaul and won some victories before, by mistake, allowing himself to be surrounded and besieged at Alesia. He was captured there and forced to throw down his arms at the feet of Caesar, who marched him in triumph through the streets of Rome in chains, threw him in prison, and had him quietly strangled.

The revenge of Vercingetorix was to succeed in becoming a hero to every young French reader of the adventures of Astérix. The series follows the struggles of Astérix and his friend Obélix in a Gaulish village as they resist Roman occupation in 50 BCE. They do so thanks to a magic potion giving them superhuman powers, brewed by the druid Panoramix, named "Getafix" in the English translation.

After the wars, you can imagine with what sense of imperial conquest Caesar entered Arles at the head of his Sixth Legion, the point of his spear. Recently, a life-size bust of him was found sunk in the Rhône, probably thrown there by his enemies after his assassination in Rome. It's a spitting image. Roman realism: a face to make men tremble, hard, deep-set eyes, a flaring nose, a boxer's hard chin, a mouth fiercely set in deathless determination. And a balding brow, where dwelt a giant's mind whose conceptions changed the world, whose commands cruelly spilled the blood of whole cities of women and children. "Enigmatic, elusive, prodigious, fathomless, he was born to conquer and seduce," as Nietzsche imagined him.

At the decisive Battle of Pharsalus, in the civil war, Caesar's cavalry was vastly outnumbered by Pompey's splendid array of brilliantly armed horsemen. Caesar devised a tactic to confound their vanity. Speaking of himself in the third person, like all dictators, he explained in his *Commentaries* [*on the Civil War*]:

> When Caesar saw the enemy's left flank so strongly supported by cavalry— the gleaming brilliance of Pompey's mounted soldiers—fearing for his army, he called up from his reserves six cohorts that he placed behind the Tenth Legion, with orders to stay quiet without showing themselves to the enemy. Instead of throwing their javelins far, as the bravest used to do, eager to come to the sword, rather he gave the order to point them straight at the visor of the helmets, and to strike the enemy in their eyes and on their face.

As Caesar explains,

> These beautiful dancers, so prettily decked out, are so eager to protect their pretty faces that they won't stand the brilliance of the iron gleaming so close to their eyes. Such was the disposition of Caesar.[2]

Blinded by their vanity—the fear that iron might mar their beauty—the enemy cavalry, despite its vastly greater numbers, was routed by Caesar's rugged veterans and by his disdainful cunning.

Caesar passed through Arles on his way to do battle against Vercingetorix. He stood right here, on my highest point, to inspect the work his soldiers were doing to erect a wall on me across the principal entry that led to Rome. He admired the view all around, rich with fertile land that stretched from the ocean to the mountains, from the Mediterranean to the little Alps as far as the eye could see. Looking for a strategic place in Gaul to locate the first Roman colony beyond the Alps, he settled on Arles, which was located on every major axis of road and river. Later, Augustus ordered the construction of a magnificent highway, the Via Apulia, that stretched at first 180 miles east from Arles as far as Nice on the way to Rome. From the west of Arles, the older Via Domitia led across the south of Gaul through the Pyrenees to the Roman colonies in Spain. Wide enough for two chariots to pass, the roads were surveyed, leveled, and paved with square stones and smooth lava. The vast interconnected system allowed armies to move quickly overland against rebellions or invasions; it facilitated trade and every kind of exotic commerce and official communication at great distances.

Remember that Caesar was also the seducer who had captivated Queen Cleopatra, the greatest beauty of the empire. Seeking to found a colony for the benefit of his hardened veterans, he didn't overlook the fact that Arlésiennes had long been celebrated for their easy ways and mysterious charms. More recently it had been said that among the women of Arles there are three types: the aristocratic women of L'Hauture with their Greek profile; the women of La Roquette, Provençal types with snub noses (*nez retroussé*); and those of a mixed type who lived near the edge of town and were most in contact with the wider world.

The Romans declared Arles and its vast territory to belong to the Roman people by right of conquest and then immediately proceeded to survey the land and divide it up into parcels that were awarded to veterans as their private property, according to their rank. Soldiers became farmers who became wealthy working the fertile territory, rich in harvests and grazing land, to feed Caesar's armies in Gaul.

As I was saying, when the Romans arrived it was a dark day for those who had lived in Arles for centuries, after the first Greek merchants from Marseille had abandoned it. The Celts were not entirely prepared to admire the civilizing influence of Rome or appreciate the honor that was being bestowed on them. But neither did they resist. They made way and accommodated the invaders, as they have mostly done through many invasions. Some very large generals controlled great tracts of land, but there were also many veterans who had grown up poor in the South of Italy and who now had the prestige and dignity of being legionnaires and enjoying the comfort of a Roman pension. Very rich Romans and a few locals had enhanced the city with gorgeous villas erected across the river in Trinquetaille, with frescoes painted by the greatest painters, brought from Rome. The villas had few windows to protect against the Midi sun; the brilliantly colored paintings served as well to light the dark interiors. Across the river became a part of Arelate once the Romans built their fabulous boat bridge to span the violent Rhône.

Augustus transformed Arelate. No expense was spared. He ordered the most precious materials, the finest marble, and the greatest artisans and painters to be brought from Italy. His architects created a coherent, unified vision of the Augustinan city, down to the smallest details of the decoration and friezes. He was determined to make his first colony across the Alps into one that resembled a "little Rome," with a forum, a theater, triumphal arches, and many temples erected to worship himself. He was thought to embody the very body of Rome itself, and in worshipping him the state was sanctified, the peace of Augustus was celebrated, and the locals received the impression of the divinely eternal permanence of imperial Roman rule. The temples of Augustus were maintained by the city as official places of sacrifice to which one came to perform the public rituals of emperor worship. It had nothing to do with any inner experience of faith or transcendence. For that, Arlesians had foreign gods, especially one secret one.

The very topmost top of me, as I've told you, has been sacred for millennia. In the place of the little Romanesque church that's there now—a hodgepodge of styles endlessly revised—once stood the adorable temple of Saturn, looking east across the great plain of La Crau to the Alps and beyond to Rome. The temple first became a primitive Christian church in the fifth century; then later this misshapen pile was grandly named Notre-Dame-la-Major because it's the oldest and most eminent one in Arles, sitting there at my highest point. Its curé was recently chased out of town for selling off the church treasures, reportedly spending the proceeds on adolescent lovers.

Saturn is one of the most ancient Roman gods, the youngest of the Twelve Titans, whose name in Greek is Cronus (not to be confused with Chronos, the god of time). Cronus castrated his father, Uranus, and in turn was overthrown by Zeus, who imprisoned him in Tartarus. Once a year for a week in December, he was free to provoke mirth and misrule. In Rome, Saturn ruled over the fields and was worshipped out of gratitude for having taught humans to cultivate the earth. He wasn't merely represented by his statue; he was thought by Romans to inhabit it. That is why, according to Favorinus, Agésilas, the king of Sparta, never wanted a statue of himself or a portrait. "It wasn't that he limped, as people say, and was short (what prevents a statue from being big and having shapely legs?) but he knew perfectly," says Favorinus, "that one must not prolong human destiny nor expose one's body to dangers on stone and bronze."[3]

The Roman veterans erected Saturn's temple up here at my top so that he might survey the surrounding countryside and keep their farms fertile, safe from flood and devastation. Just as in Rome, Arles kept the public treasury in Saturn's temple because the titan and his partner Ops, goddess of opulence, were said to belong to that golden age of abundance that Romans associated with wealth that was held in common, for the common good, before there was private property. As Lucian of Samosata wrote, "All things grew without sowing or plowing of the earth—not just ears of corn, but loaves complete and meat ready cooked—when wine flowed in rivers, and there were fountains of milk and honey, all men were good, and all men were gold. When Cronus was king, slavery was not, the slave and the free as one."[4] So, on December 17, when Saturnalia begins, they untie the woolen threads that bind the feet of the statue of Saturn on the Capitoline in Rome; it marks the beginning of the festivities: Saturn himself is now free to join the dance.

Saturn was above all beloved of slaves, during the Saturnalia, when they were free to sit at table with their masters, to call them names (in good fun—let none be wounded), and like them to wear only a short tunic (no toga necessary for the orgies). Rich shall not send gifts to rich or entertain peers at the feast. During the week of his festival, Saturn orders that all shall be equal, slave and free, rich, and poor, one with another. No one in these days shall count his money, or inspect her wardrobe, or make an inventory. Athletic training shall cease. No discourse shall be either composed or delivered, except it be witty and lusty, promoting mirth and gaiety. All seriousness is barred; no business is allowed, except that of cooks and bakers. Drinking, and being drunk, noise and games and dice, appointing of kings and feasting of slaves, singing naked, clapping excitedly, an occasional dunking of corked faces in icy water.

This festival at the beginning of winter was the world turned upside down, in which everyone changes places and changes gender. Men act like women and vice versa; women lend themselves to male pleasures with abandon; masters take orders from their slaves, even play dice with them. Arlesians love a feria, and the Saturnalia was the wildest one of all as people faced down the coming bitter winter, nervously eyeing the stock of food they had carefully gathered and stored at the harvest. They ate more and drank much more than was prudent, defying all restraints. People danced in the street or at wild parties, yelling, "Io, Saturnalia," in each other's face. At the end of every summer, the population of Arles jumped—noticeably.

On the steps of the temple of Saturn was the altar to a different god, who had no name, no face or figure, who was called Bona Dea, the good goddess. Her altar was miraculously found intact when they were digging in front of Notre-Dame-la-Major. Some say Bona Dea is a secret name for Cybele because her altar, which can be seen even today at the museum, is engraved with a beribboned oak-leaf wreath sacred to Cybele. Both are mother goddesses of wild nature, and Arles was for millennia a farm town thick with aurochs. In place of a figure or face, the center of the oak wreath is empty—except for two beautifully shaped ears (!) sculpted right and left, as if to tell her adepts that the goddess, though invisible, is listening. Bona Dea is one of the listening goddesses, absent but attentive to prayers. Her followers are largely women, and it was mainly noblewomen who organized her festivities. But not only noblewomen: her altar's priestess was a freed slave. Her festivities were celebrated on the first of May, when aristocratic women in town gathered at the home of the wife of the consul to commemorate the dedication of Dea's temple in Rome. All signs of maleness, man or animal, were erased from the premises. Even statues of noblemen were covered. The festival allowed women to lend themselves without scandal to the most outrageous behavior. They drank strong wines ordinarily forbidden to them, from jugs they called honey pots (*mellarium*); they called the wine in them "milk" (*lac*) and drank to get drunk. They renamed the wine forbidden to them to hide it from themselves, while they drank to excess and dared to gamble. They used the vilest language with one another, cursing and telling filthy jokes to gales of laughter. "Hey, Mellissa, shoot me some of your lac." It was all very naughty but chaste, shunning husbands, even the noblest—even Venus herself: of all the leaves and flowers that decorated the house of the matrons for the holiday, only myrtle was forbidden. Myrtle is sacred to Aphrodite, who was supposed to be absent from the male-less precincts of the festival. It was rather a way of celebrating the role of matrons, on whose fertility the society depends, without endangering the order of inheritance and rule. And for a moment of the year, the mothers can act like nymphs, wild and unattached, and free themselves among themselves from the yoke of male domination.

Nearby, up here on me, the women came with the priestess of Bona Dea to sacrifice a pig in her honor and throw its carcass in a pit. They then retrieved what was left of last year's rotten carcass and gave it to the rich farmers for their crops, an infallible guarantee of human fertility and cereal abundance from the good goddess herself.

Of course, the good goddess could also be me, the Rock of Arles, of whom there can be no statue. You can't make a statue of that on which the pedestal stands. I am invisible but under every foot, and all around. I listen to every prayer, whispering to some, forgetting nothing. Since the Greeks from Marseille first set up shop on me 2,600 years ago, business in Arles has had its ups and downs—for a long time, mostly down. There's hope now that the city is being reborn, as it has been so many times before after decline and defeat and destruction. Founded by Caesar, the city of Augustus, little Rome, once the capital of all of Gaul, is beginning again to rise out of darkness to its former eminence.

"O Arles," Mistral cried, "O you who has been everything that one can be, the metropolis of an empire, the capital of a kingdom, the mother of Liberty." ("*O toi qui a été tout ce que l'on peut être, la métrople d'un empire, la capital d'un royaume, la mere de la liberté.*")[5] May you soon return to that estate from which you had fallen so far but to which your glorious ruins attest, as you assume your place among cities as a model of equality, a fount of truth, and a beacon of free thought—a harbinger of the future of cities.

To the city and to the world I want to bring the wisdom of Favorinus, Arles's greatest mind. A lowly Celt, befriended by the emperor, with no Roman blood, he spoke in unimaginably eloquent Greek about the universality of Hellenist civilization. He promoted what the Greeks called *paideia*, a universal system of education, of physical and mental training, including sports and dance, science and poetry, literature and philosophy, with the aim of producing a fully cultivated, harmonious human being.

For Favorinus, paidea is a system, he says in his letter to the Corinthians, open to all and of value to everyone. Speaking on behalf of the statue of himself, once erected in Corinth, now missing, Favorinus affirms the mission for which he seems to have been born, as if destined by the gods, to bring the good news of paideia to all the peoples of the empire, taking himself as a prime example of what marvels it can achieve. Among Greeks, he is a Roman who speaks Greek better than they do—a fact that leads them to question the so-called superiority of Greece to Rome. It proves to them that you don't have to have been born in Greece to acquire fame in Greek oratory. Romans get so wrapped up in their own reputation that they neglect the education they require to deserve that reputation. And for the Celts, "barbarians" like Favorinus himself, he serves as an example to them of how they need not reject paideia but ought to acquire it for their fame and fortune. Favorinus, after all, was entitled to the position of knight (*eques*), and Hadrian wanted to make him the high priest in his temple in Arles. Only the richest and highest-placed Romans could aspire to such a charge, one that Favorinus, at the risk of everything, declined.

Favorinus sees himself as a missionary to the Corinthians, reminding them of the value of their accumulated wisdom. At a time when all around him other religions were burgeoning, with their exclusive dogmas, above all Christianity, Favorinus lent his oratory to celebrating the cosmopolitan, humanist, scientific, and philosophical greatness of Greek and Roman culture—the beauty and wisdom of Greco-Roman Hellenism.

Favorinus died an old man late in the second century during the reign of Emperor Antonius Pius. In his will he bestowed his great library on his dearest friend, the philosopher Herod Atticus, the wealthy benefactor of Athens. The library doubtless contained the summits of Greek and Roman thought—art, history, science, and philosophy. He himself wrote more than two hundred books on an immense array of subjects. Most of the books are lost, only titles remain, and fragments quoted here and there in other writers. He wrote on Socrates and his conception of the art of love, "In Praise of the Quarter Fever of Malaria," "On Old Age," "For the Defense of the Baths," "The Conduct of Philosophers," "On Prayer," "The Forms," "The Philosophy of Homer."

It was the universality of the empire itself—collecting an immense diversity of people under the overarching rule of Roman law—that made it possible to dream of universal, encyclopedic knowledge that could be available to all people. But not without the discipline of serious study and application. Favorinus was above all a teacher, who had schools and disciples in Athens and Corinth and Rome.

At that the Rock paused. I took the opportunity to run upstairs, and when I returned, I waited a long time before deciding the Rock had had enough for the day.

IV

Venus Genetrix

The next day I again waited a long time, but as I was about to leave, the Rock began, abruptly, to continue where it had left off:

The first thing the Romans built were walls, fortifications that encircled me at the top and to which the people retreated up my sides whenever invasion threatened. Next, they built at my foot an enormous Roman forum, three football fields long, half of it on flat ground, half on a terrace dug into my side at the bottom of my hill. The engineers had to invent a complicated foundation to even out the radical difference in height between the flat land at my foot and me. The terrace they dug was the first of many deep cuts I received from the Romans, who had no sense of the Earth and saw in me only a canvas on which to project their brilliant monuments. Nothing remains of the immense Roman forum in Arles, except for some foundation stones and two Corinthian columns, late additions, now fronting the paltry Place du Forum. Arelate was full of temples erected to honor Augustus, the first emperor to declare himself to be a god. He might well have been one, as far as Arles was concerned. Caesar, merely a dictator who ended the Republic, founded the colony; Augustus built it. It took the Romans about three hundred years before they were finished: the last great monument, the enormous public baths built by Constantine, in time became an emperor's palace.

IV.1. The shaded stage of the antique theater

Next, up my hill, came a more important wound in my side, a vast terrace on which was built the antique Roman theater. It had no roof but was entirely enclosed behind walls, on the model of Pompey's first stone theater, built a few years before in Rome. It had retractable sails in case of rain. It seated ten thousand, compared with twenty thousand in the arena, built sixty years later. The theater was situated halfway up my side along the *decumanus*, the main east-west axis, overlooking the whole town and dominating the political and civic spaces. Citizens frequently assembled there for civic ceremonies, as well as entertainment. It's where many of the local Celts first learned Latin.

The stage, fifty meters long and six meters wide, was laid with the finest Carrara marble, brought from Italy over the sea and up the Rhône by flat-bottom boats. The hundreds of shimmering colored marble columns, on three levels, that composed the scenic wall at the back of the stage were intended to evoke the grandeur of the emperor's palace on the Palatine Hill in Rome. Only two giant pillars have survived the centuries and the depredation of Christians who considered it a "temple of false gods" and stole its stones for successive versions of their cathedral. Enough remains that lets one imagine the extraordinary wealth expended by the emperor to quietly impress upon the barbarians the fact of Roman power and the glorious advent of imperial dignity.

The orchestra, the semicircular space in front of the front row of seats, reserved for knights and nobles, was floored in swirling cipollino-like marble, pale green, edged in wide pink bands of Breccia made of large, colored marble stones embedded inside a marble matrix. It's there on the orchestra that the chorus evolved and assumed its places. In the center was an altar dedicated to Apollo, not Dionysus, the customary god of theaters. Behind it, in a niche in the front of the stage, was another little altar, with the god himself at rest with his lyre, leaning against his Delphic tripod and flanked by laurel trees. Augustus saw Apollo as the god of the sun, his own tutelary deity, the one who protects princes like him and gave him his great victory at Actium against Marc Antony and Cleopatra.

The masked actors were slaves or freed slaves. The minute an actor stepped on stage, like gladiators in the arena, he (there were very few women) lost all his civil rights. Actors in comedies wore clownish masks: hooked noses, big ears, gaping mouths to play the angry father, a rascal slave, a boastful soldier, a brothel madam, the ogre Mandacus, or his wife, the ogress Lamia. In pantomime, the actor/dancer wore a mask with the mouth closed, and a chorus offstage sang and read the texts. In tragedies, the actors put on tragic masks with open mouths, which expressed the feelings or the temper of the persona; the masks were changed as actors assumed different roles. The young heroine and the brave hero wore idealized masks.

In the theater, hierarchies were rigidly enforced. The seating was divided into three separate sections, each with its own door, to prevent the mingling of classes: knights and nobles were seated below in the orchestra, the people higher up in the stands. Loose women and slaves were at the very top. The system of exclusion required the most amazing architectural solutions by Roman engineers to direct the spectators by their class.

In this theater/temple, people came not only to be entertained but also to worship the emperor, the embodiment of the state. Worship, mainly in the form of sacrifice, was part of the public religion that served to affirm and reinforce Roman order. A colossal statue of Augustus towered over all from a vast height, ensconced in a niche, looking down on lesser gods whose statues peopled the stage below him. His statue up there on high, ten feet tall, still stands in the middle of the antiquity museum in Arles. He is still magnificently erect, with a vast molded chest swollen with Roman pride and a head—once cut, now recovered—of such commanding beauty that it drove Arlesian women (and many men) mad with imperial piety.

On either side of the statue of Augustus were two incomparably beautiful figures of Venus. One was Venus Victrix, first so-called by Pompey, then by Caesar at Pharsalus, where he defeated his rival in her name, the goddess of high-spirited eros in love and war. She held a helmet, a small oval shield (a *clipeus*), and a spear. "Venus Victrix" was also the battle cry he gave his soldiers. Victrix was also the name of the Sixth Legion, to which Caesar donated Arles. Framing her, on the other side, in her own niche, was another even more dazzling statue, one of Venus Genetrix, the new name Caesar gave her when he erected a temple in Rome in her honor. She was intended to remind Arles that Augustus, adopted son of Caesar, owed his authority to Venus, the divine ancestor of the gens Julia. Her son, the Trojan Aeneas, founded Rome before Romulus and Remus.

Augustus, like Macron, saw himself as Jupiter on high, invested with sacred power. But it was Venus who was most beloved by Caesar and by Augustus as well. The most distinguished Roman families for some time had found it appealing to claim a divine origin. Iulus, the mythical ancestor claimed by Caesar, was another name for Ascanius, the son of Aeneas, immortalized by Virgil, which is derived from *iulus*, meaning "woolly worm." Aeneas, in turn, was the son of Venus-Aphrodite and the mortal Trojan hero Anchise. Romans were eager to claim Trojan ancestry. Caesar refers often to the divine origins of the gens Julia. Having been declared an enemy of the state, Caesar had political reasons for claiming to have descended from the founder of Rome.

In the theater, attracting all the light, the gleaming white statue of Venus Genetrix stood larger than life, carved from the purest milky marble brought from Thassos, looking like she had stepped directly from the hand of Praxiteles—a dream of Greek loveliness, the most beautiful statue of a woman ever made in Roman Gaul. She's now in the Louvre. Her lovely, small-featured face turns down to see herself in the mirror she probably held below in her left hand. Her right arm is raised, perhaps about to touch her hair. The gesture opens her half-naked form to full view of her unspeakably gorgeous belly. She was found buried beneath the orchestra of the theater, missing arms that were never found. For years, the Arlesians debated her identity. Books were written; arguments raged. Some thought she was Venus; others were convinced she was the goddess Diana. It also mattered to these lovers of antiquity whether the ruins were those of a theater or a temple. Diana loved sacrifices in blood, even human sacrifices, it was rumored. Books were written disputing the claims. The matter was decided by Louis XIV, passing through Arles, who declared she was Venus and so admired the statue that he suggested to the city fathers that they might like to make him a gift of her for his new chateau at Versailles. They weren't pleased to lose their most beautiful ancient artifact.

Louis commissioned his sculptor Girardon to provide her with missing arms. He put a mirror in one hand and in the other a small golden apple, the prize for beauty that she fatefully won from the hand of Paris. Arlesians came to the theater to see and to adore her beauty. The worship of beautiful women in Arles probably began there with the Venus of Arles. Arlésiennes have been celebrated for centuries in music, painting, and fiction. Even today, women and young girls, devoted to preserving the culture of Provence, parade around town during the ferias in the rich materials of the traditional Arlésienne costume, whose hourglass shape—with hair upswept, elegantly crowned with ribbon—uncannily makes all women beautiful. They are not only beautiful but harmonious in the way they inhabit their dress, reflecting feelings of deep reverence for the past. Perfectly at ease in this costume that has been passed down in families and meticulously re-created, the Arlésiennes, strangely familiar, familiarly strange, seem otherworldly as they stroll around town, as if stepped uncannily out of another century. Every year they elect one of their number to be the queen of Arles. After being crowned in the ancient theater at a great public ceremony, she sits with her court next to the mayor at the corrida, in front of brave men in tight pants all in gold who kill bulls—often splendidly. When they do, Beauty receives the ear of the bull from the hand of its killer still dripping with Blood. The bloody ear always reminds me of the one Van Gogh cut off and gave to Rachel in the bordello in Arles, as if he were at once himself both the bull and the swordsman.

These Arlésiennes acquire their costume and their culture from their affiliation with the *félibrige*, the society founded by seven poets in 1854, chief among them Frédéric Mistral, with the aim to promote and codify Provençal; the language is one of the many spoken dialects of Old Occitan, the classical language in which troubadours across Europe in the twelfth and thirteenth centuries wrote their lyric cansos. In the year 1800, 70 percent of the population in Arles spoke Provençal; by 1850, it had all but disappeared, as the city transitioned from agriculture to industry.

IV.2. Three
Arlesian graces
from the back

The félibrige came to the rescue of this language and its habits just as it was about to vanish. The association required its members to practice Provençal. Mistral himself produced a French-Provençal dictionary, *Lou Tresor dou Félibrige*, in order to codify its spelling. It caught the musical ear of the great Romantic poet Lamartine, who wrote Mistral to praise "*Ce doux et nerveux idiome provençal qui rappelle, tantôt l'accent latin, tantôt la grâce attique, tantôt l'âpreté toscane. . . .*"[1] ("This sweet and edgy idiom of Provençal that at times recalls the accent of Latin, sometimes attic grace, sometimes Tuscan harshness. . . .") Sweet and edgy: a graceful vocalic rhythm made nervous by the abrupt punctuation of harsh consonants. Mistral encouraged his fellow poets, in Paris and elsewhere, to produce literary works, which they did in great numbers. He himself wrote an enormously popular epic poem, *Mirèio* (in French, *Mirelle*) about the hopeless love of two peasants from different classes—with echoes of Shakespeare. His greatest work, "Le poème du Rhône," celebrates the past of the Rhône when it was the bustling artery of all the commerce from Lyon to the Mediterranean. The poem bemoans the loss of the vibrant, heroic life of those who plied their trade on the river, before steam engines and railroads changed everything.

The félibrige is the association created by Mistral to preserve the rural culture of the early nineteenth century in the face of its imminent disappearance. That's why its members adopt the language, costume, and values of a society more rural than urban, more rooted in the life of the Camargue than the turbulence of Arles. It gave rise to a world whose nostalgia for a vanished past has often lent itself to being exploited by the politics of blood and soil.

Favorinus wrote a text of which we have only the title, *For the Defense of Gladiators*. He wrote it at a time when his friend the emperor Hadrian was building arenas all over the empire, sponsoring games and sometimes, fully armed, deigning to combat in the arena. Hadrian understood how the wild popularity of gladiator games could diffuse and redirect popular passions. As they used to say, *panem et circenses*, bread and circuses, were the emperor's principal bribes for securing the people's affection. Moralists of every stripe at the time condemned the games for their cruelty and inhumanity. Gladiators were classed among those labeled *infames*, people of bad reputation, ranked alongside or below actors, prostitutes, pimps, and bankrupts as social and moral outcasts, unworthy of decent burial. They could not vote, plead in court, or leave a will, and unless they were released from service, their lives and property belonged to their masters.

To defend them, I've heard Favorinus extol the model of courage they personify, their fierce impassive resignation to the prospect of their imminent death. The spectacle they provide, like the corrida in Arles, opens one's eyes to the seriousness of life, bringing to everyday experience the possibility of looking death in the face—the very instant of death: the moment when the flame goes out. When a heroic bull has fought and died well, he is celebrated by the crowd with *vueltas*, turns around the arena to standing applause in gratitude for the gift his death has purveyed. Along with *mucho dinero* for those who produce the spectacle. The odor of manure that hangs over the arena has the smell of money: filthy lucre.

Arles has kept the tradition of killing the bull, uninterrupted since the nineteenth century, a fact that gives it the legal right to do what is forbidden in most of the rest of France, where it has been only intermittently practiced, as in Paris. The corrida reminds the city that it is founded no less on blood

IV.3. Mistral and friends in the Place du Forum

than on beauty, no less on beauty than blood—like the stripes on the city's first flag, alternating blood and gold, as on the Catalan flag, only horizontal. In 1793 blood of its citizens ran in the streets of Arles when the republicans down in La Roquette, near the river, attacked the nobles in their *hôtels* higher up on my sides. The double side of Arles has often led to fratricidal political combat. *Urbs dupleix*—everything about the city since antiquity has been double. *Sang et or*, blood and beauty, beauty and blood.

When the torero rises up and plunges his sword over the horns of the bull into the hump on its back, if he does it perfectly, he will cut an aorta and the bull instantly falls down dead. If he kills correctly, his own neck passes over one of the horns as he shifts to the side to avoid the charge. In that instant of absolute danger, if the bull were to raise its powerful head, the matador would die. The spectacle of absolute danger from the safety of a spectator's seat produces, if it is done well, the very definition of a sublime aesthetic experience. That dangerous beauty has come to feel even more necessary in a city now in some danger of drowning in a flood of foreign tourists, who in summer engulf my streets.

August in Arles, and *aficionados* go to the bullfights at the little arena in Saintes-Maries-de-la-Mer, its beach town in the Camargue where the delta meets the Mediterranean. It was there, after the death of the Virgin Mary, that the three holy Marys, disciples of Jesus, fleeing Roman rule, came ashore from Jerusalem to begin the missionary work of Christianizing pagan Gaul. One who arrived was Mary Magdalene, the sister of Lazarus, said by some to be the wife of Jesus, the first to see him after he was resurrected; she came along with two other disciples, Marie Salomé, the sister of the Virgin Mary, and Mary Jacoby, either another sister or a cousin of the Virgin. In May of every year, Roms in their gypsy caravans from all over Europe gather on the beach of Saintes Maries-de-la-Mer to walk their black Virgin back into the sea. In truth, she may have been no virgin. She's the saintly Sara Kali, from either Egypt or, more likely, India, who after converting to Christianity became the servant of the three Marys. Outcast Gypsies venerate the black servant even above her mistresses. It's with her image that they bless the Mediterranean. Ask any gypsy to name the three Marys and she will intone: "Mary Salomé, Mary Jacoby, and Mary Sara."

With that, the Rock grew silent. I was about to get up to go when I was star-tled to hear the Rock address me by name:

Don't you think I know, Richárd, that you've been skipping classes and coming to Arles twice a year for the bullfights. I know too, of course, that you had lost your aficion and have lately recovered it, somewhat diminished. You came to loathe the moment when the ridiculous matador, squeezed into gold pants, ass and bulge protruding, stands aside the fallen hero smiling broadly, chin upraised, arms outstretched in triumph, beseeching the crowd for the tro-phy of a bloody ear, while this suberb animal sprawled in a pool of its blood vomits its tongue. And the mob erupts. Is it the cruelty that brings you back or what St. Augustine calls "*libidine sanguis*"?

I couldn't answer. I really didn't know. I got up and went upstairs.

Urbs Genesii

It's September, and I'm back in our house, here for the Feria du Riz. It's the festival that recognizes the role that the rice harvest has played in the economy of Arles for the past 150 years. At the end of the nineteenth century, after the phylloxera aphid had wiped out French vines, rice was planted in fields that were drowned in fresh water from the Rhône—not for its own sake but to allow the cultivation of other crops in a delta soil that would otherwise be too salty for agriculture. The only vines able to resist the devastation of the insect were those whose roots were planted in water. On the eve of World War II, the cultivation of rice had all but ceased. Things changed in 1942, when the supply of cheap rice from the French colonies was cut off, and farmers thought to exploit the Camargue for its boundless supply of fresh water.

The weather was unusually warm, so when the sun came up, I went down to the cool of the cave. After a while I wasn't too surprised when the Rock began to speak of Castilla, who I was seeing that afternoon, fighting the Iberian combat bulls of Yonnet, the first to be bred in the Camargue. Their bulls are not nearly as big and fierce as the dreaded Miura, but they are smart and fast, and can whip around after a pass before the torero has a chance to turn his back and step aside from the slashing horns. The Rock described the scene with the precise attention of a real aficionado:

I've been observing gladiator games on my shoulder for more than two thousand years, except for a period of Christian occupation. I naturally have my favorites among the current cohort of French toreros. I can remember every moment of their *suerte*. These days I most admire Castilla, a subtle silver thread of a killer. Last April, even I was amazed as I watched him arch his body around the repeatedly charging bull, while his feet, unmoving, were rooted in place. Soon the obedient animal began to follow every movement of the *muletta*, as if on a string. Everywhere Castilla sent him he went with lowered head. The torero synchronized the movement of the bull with the rhythm of the cape in endless-seeming waves that would have brought tears to my eyes if rocks could cry at the beauty of it all—at the heart-stopping serenity of the coordinated rhythm of man and beast and veil. After a while the crowd began to cry, *"Indulto! Indulto!"* Pardon, pardon the bull! Sparing the bull is done with the greatest reluctance, for killing the bull is the whole point of the combat. The torero is finally judged on how well he performs the coup de grâce. After a long hesitation, while the public clamors for mercy, the judges finally wave the orange handkerchief that signals pardon for the bull (as if it were a criminal needing forgiveness). The bullfighter mimes a kill, and as happens very rarely, the bull is led off by a belled troupe of steers and condemned to spend the rest of his days in rich pastures among pliant cows.

The corrida illustrates what I would call the art of cruelty. The word attests to the heartless sadism of the corrida, but it recalls as well *cruor*—Latin for "blood," specifically, the bloody gore that flows from an open wound. Unless the gratuitous putting to death of a great, beautiful, intelligent beast offends you, the blinding vision of an intensely bright sun reflected off the vast, blood-soaked back of a combat bull will lead you to understand why bulls in antiquity were sacred to Apollo, the sun god, and hence beloved of the emperor. Augustus had carved bulls' heads posted all around his theater in Arles.

Combat bulls have horizontal horns, whereas those of Camargue bulls are vertical, shaped like a lyre. They are never killed in the arena but reappear year after year in *courses camarguaises*, local bull games, when brave young men, all in white with a red bandana, boldly rush at the bulls armed with a sort of comb to snatch a ribbon, a tassel, or a cockade attached to their horns. Sometimes the *razeurs* are caught from behind as they leap over the barriers to flee the horns aimed to do harm. The bulls that return to fight in the arena grow smarter year after year; some become celebrities whose names attract crowds.

V.1. Castella gives the coup de grâce

V.2. Roman brickwork in the arena

Ninety years after they gouged out the theater, the Romans dug an even vaster terrace in my side to install the arena, only the second in the empire after the Coliseum in Rome. When the first was inaugurated, Emperor Titus allowed one hundred days of festivities and five thousand savage beasts to be killed in a single day. Here in Arles they were obliged to remove part of the city wall to make room for an arena of thirty thousand spectators, with cellars for gladiators and many wild beasts. The amphitheater and its bloody spectacle played an important role in the life of the army, which in turn upheld the values of the civic religion with unfailing vitality till about the beginning of the fourth century. Soldiers who witnessed the savage games were obliged to sacrifice to the imperial gods and observe rites before attending bloody spectacles. To the emperor's power of judging was added that of putting criminals to death for the well-being and preservation of the citizens. Prisoners of war who were sacrificed in the arena betokened the pacifying virtue of spilled blood. The public took a lively pleasure in seeing criminals torn to pieces by wild animals.

Eusebius, a fourth-century Christian propagandist, recounts how one of the martyrs in the time of the Great Persecutions was brought before the governor and commanded to sacrifice to the imperial Roman gods. As he refused, he was raised up on high and beaten with rods over his entire body. He was unmoved by his suffering, even though his bones were already appearing; they mixed vinegar with salt and poured it upon the mangled parts of his body. As he scorned these agonies, a gridiron and fire were brought forward. The remnants of his body, like flesh intended for eating, were placed on the fire, not at once, lest he should expire instantly, but a little at a time. But he held his purpose firmly and victoriously gave up his life while the tortures were still going on. Such was the martyrdom of one of the victims, who was indeed well worthy of his name, which was Peter. In Lyon they dragged a Christian woman into the arena, beat her, and forced her to sit on the iron chair until the smell of her grilled flesh perfumed the arena. Only then was she blessedly immolated. I'm reminded of when Athenians thought to vote to establish gladiator games in rivalry with Corinth; Anaximander admonished them that if they passed the law in favor of the games, they ought to destroy the city's altar to the goddess Pity.

When Christians began persecuting pagans, they were at least as cruel. Hypatia of Alexandria was one of the most accomplished astronomers and mathematicians in antiquity, who also happened to be a woman. In the fourth century the city was a great center of Hellenistic studies, with one of the largest libraries in the ancient world. Only books written in Greek were admitted; non-Greek books had first to be translated. With her father, Theon, a distinguished astronomer, Hypatia wrote commentaries on the mathematical astronomy of Ptolemy, on the geometry of Apollonius and Diophantus. She considered herself above all to be a philosopher, whose seminars on Plato and Aristotle attracted admiring crowds from around the empire, Christian as well as pagan. She disputed the dominant neo-Platonic readings of Plotinus, with their airy speculations, in favor of what appears to have been a more severe and strictly logical understanding of Plato. She had no interest in the Greek and Roman mythologies, in their gods and cults. She was tolerant of Christians but disdained their religion. She was universally praised for what the Greeks called her *sophrosuné*: excellence of character and soundness of mind that leads to temperance, moderation, prudence, purity, decorum, and self-control. Hypatia was as beautiful as she was brilliant. But she remained a virgin her entire life. She was ascetic to the point that some have called her a Cynic philosopher [*from the Greek* kuon, *"dog"*] because she despised the body. The Ideal that Cynic philosophers contemplate was understood to be so far superior to any finite, material thing that the body, by comparison, was nothing—lower than nothing, worthy only of the attention of dogs—as she used to say, "a pile of shit." When she walked around the city, she often wore a simple *tribon*, a rough cloth cloak that Greeks threw around themselves, especially philosophers. When a student confessed his love for her, she famously showed him her bloody sanitary napkin. "This is what you are in love with, nothing of the good is here."

Hypatia was one of the principal exponents of Euclidean geometry and wrote commentaries on the principles of algebra and astronomy. Her scientific and philosophical interests attracted a large crowd of disciples, many of high birth, educated and wealthy, who sought to study with her. She was not beloved of the masses in Alexandria, from whom she remained detached and disdainful. Her teaching of sophisticated philosophical argument was reserved for her elect disciples.

She incurred the jealous rage of the Christian patriarch of Alexandria, who observed the gorgeous train of horses and chariots surrounding her house belonging to the rich and powerful who came from all over the empire to study with her. Frequented by imperial dignitaries and others of high rank, she was a highly esteemed citizen and influential adviser to the government. The archbishop Cyril, impetuous and power hungry, was relentless in his pursuit of it. He was above all determined to counter the influence that Hypatia exerted over Orestes, the Roman prefect who ruled the city. Orestes, baptized in Constantinople before becoming governor of Alexandria, was accused by Christians of being a secret pagan. One day, as he was riding through the city, he was confronted by a group of fanatical monks under the direction of the archbishop. He was insulted and bloodied by a stone-throwing monk. Orestes struggled with Cyril to recover the powers the archbishop had usurped from the Roman authorities. Hypatia was a friend and adviser. She was despised by the Christians for her learning and philosophical distinction and for her influence on the governor. She returned their hatred with contempt for their ridiculous superstition.

A rumor spread that the daughter of Theon was the only obstacle in the way of reconciliation between the prefect and the archbishop. On a holy day in the season of Lent, Cyril unleashed the Christian populace against her. Pointing to her astronomical devices, he encouraged rumors that she was a witch who practiced sorcery and satanic arts of divination. He incited a group of monks and minor clergy, crazed with fasting and religious fervor, to form a band with the intention of killing the woman philosopher, "the pagan woman." His tonsured hounds, followed by a mob of fanatics, led by a lector named Peter (*eh, oui*), savagely attacked Hypatia in the street, dragged her by the hair from her chariot, stripped her naked, and threw her into one of the principal churches. On the altar they cut her to pieces with shards of broken tile, scraped the flesh from her bones, then took away her body, shamefully treated, to be grilled, still quivering. Can anything be more horrible and cowardly than the conduct of the priests of this bishop, whom Christians style Saint Cyril, who uttered no word of reprimand?

It took Christians less than a hundred years to go from the tolerance of Constantine legitimizing Christianity to the intolerance of Emperor Theodosius, who banned all pagan practices, on pain of death. Extermination was the Christians' solution to dispatching their opponents; they couldn't rest until they were rid of pagans entirely. They undertook what Gibbon calls "a singular event in the history of the human mind," the only example of "the total extirpation of ancient and popular superstitions."[1] It still astounds me that within a hundred years or so, Christianity, as the sole and exclusive religion of the empire, replaced all the myriad cults that had thrived for centuries, as well as the official state religion. There are those who say that proves it is the only true religion; others say it's because it's the most intolerant. For the pope, there are no alternative paths to salvation. That is why Christians have a special obligation to evangelize, to preach conversion in the name of the one Truth, and that is Jesus. Even Jews, alone among the Roman cults who claimed to be specially chosen by God—even they allowed righteous Gentiles a share in the happiness of the afterlife, a place "in the world to come [העולם הבא]." They need only to have obeyed the seven laws God gave to Noah (prohibiting blasphemy, idolatry, adultery, bloodshed, theft, and eating the blood of a living animal) before Moses brought a few more from Sinai. *[They also included the positive injunction "to establish laws."]* In heaven, the happiness of righteous Gentiles was naturally not expected to compare to that of pious Jews, who in their lifetime had obeyed all 613 *mitzvot* commanded in Genesis and Deuteronomy. Yet Christians were even more exclusive. The Church decided early on that outside of it there was no half-way to heaven—no salvation without baptism: "The Roman Empire excludes from its tolerance only the intolerant." Christianity includes in its intolerance every form of religious tolerance.

Christian nationalists in America say that if Jesus had had an AR-15, he would not have been crucified. But if he had had an AR-15, he would not have been Jesus. That might lead you to think that Christian nationalism is an oxymoron. The warlike patriotism of nationalists, their dreams of violence, their fondness for militias, would seem to be at odds with the aims of the Prince of Peace. But since the fourth century, Christianity has been allied to the power of political princes of every stripe. Christian nationalists since Theodosis and his son have ultimately given the pagans, the non-Christians, a choice of exile, forced conversion, or extermination.

As I was starting to say about the arena: gladiators generally died young, but not all. The slave Primus Asiaticus, the great star of combats at Arelate, racked up fifty-three victories before he was finally freed and allowed to die a peaceful death. Gladiators adopted names to reflect their strength or physical qualities. They called themselves Ursius (strong as a bear), Fulgur (lightning), Ferax (fearless), Calidromus (the quick one), or Callimorphus (well-built). Many were the tombs of gladiators erected by their feminine admirers, wives or concubines, tokens of their success with women.

The *lanista* was the one who trained gladiators to fight and taught them their art. He was frequently an ex-gladiator who carried a wand as a mark of authority. Sometimes he was the owner of a band of gladiators, mostly slaves, whom he praised to rich or powerful patrons who could afford to sponsor the spectacles; more often it was the fencing master who exercised control of the state-owned companies, like Marcus Julius Olympus, the most celebrated lanista at Arles. He had a troop of Celtic gladiators that were renowned around the empire for their barbaric cruelty toward man and beast. Gladiators, like Emperor Commodus, identified with Hercules and Mars, and with Dionysus too, because his chariot was attached to wild animals he had tamed. Nemesis, the evil goddess of vengeance, was much beloved by gladiators. She was also a goddess of death, particularly sudden or accidental death. There were many altars to Nemesis, who incarnated victory and happy completion.

On the walls of the arena, you can still see scrawled the name of Mithras, the principal god of gladiators and soldiers. He was Phrygian, from Anatolia in Turkey, whose cult turned around his killing Taurus, a cosmic bull. He was worshiped in a *mithraeum*, built underground to resemble the cave in which the god was born. A magnificent head of Mithras, now in the museum in Arles, came from the ruins of one of several *mithraea* down by the Rhône. In the center of the underground, vaulted mithraeum was an altar with benches on either side. On it was depicted the god, looking Persian in his Phrygian cap, the top curled down in front; it was the cap worn by French revolutionaries, who thought they were reliving the ancient revolt of Phrygian slaves led by Spartacus. Mithras sits astride the bull, wielding a dagger at its heart, while a dog barks, probably the star Canis, and a water snake, the constellation Hydra, hisses at its feet. A scorpion, who must be the cosmic Scorpius, tries to sting the bull's balls. They are all friends of Mithras, who is stabbing away. He himself is also Helios, the sun god, in the constellation Leo. This killing of the bull, this tauroctony, reenacts the combat of bulls and lions in the arena. The whole myth has cosmic significance about the coming of a new age, promising salvation to its adepts on a higher plane.

For a few centuries, the religion of Mithras spread across the empire, promoted by legionaries—in direct competition with early Christianity. Jesus and Mithras offered the people, even the lowliest, a chance of salvation. In the first centuries of the Common Era, Mithras had as many followers as Jesus, until Christianity, with the help of princes, eradicated him in the fourth century. In the end he lost out to the god from Bethlehem as the Roman army dissolved.

It was on the altar of the mithraeum that a bull was often sacrificed and the gladiators, stripped naked, bathed in its blood to give them courage. Sometimes they bathed in a pit of blood from a bull sacrificed on a grill overhead. The blood of the bull, pouring down, not only lent valor to the gladiators but also promised salvation to the soldiers who also drank the blood and ate the flesh. Sometimes they only mimed the tauroctony.

Some say Mithras, born a god a hundred years earlier, may have anticipated Jesus. Like him he was born on December 25, wrapped in swaddling clothes, placed in a manger, and attended by shepherds. He had twelve companions or "disciples" and was viewed as the Good Shepherd, "the Way, the Truth and the Light," the Redeemer, the Savior, the Messiah. He was identified with both the Lion and the Lamb. His sacred day was Sunday, "the Lord's Day." His religion had a eucharistic ritual or "Lord's Supper," eating the flesh and drinking the blood of the god. It eventually lost out to Christianity because it also excluded women, who were, therefore, in great numbers, the first Christian converts in Arles.

Mithras is linked to the Iranian god of the sun by the same name, but he became in Rome a god of the heavens, surrounded by stars, who kills the bull so that a new age can be born: the Age of Aries, which precedes Taurus in the zodiac but follows it in time. The next precession, when the constellations shift in the sky, sometime in the next hundred years, will usher in the Age of Aquarius that precedes us in the Age of Pisces but will follow on next. The soul of the worshipper rose through celestial heavens to dwell in some ethereal unity with the cosmos.

By the second century, Mithras was already being replaced in the arena by bloody images of Diana, the huntress. Her cult was practiced with human sacrifice, it's said, but that's a lie told by Christians. The story goes that it was St. Trophime, the first archbishop of Arles, who heard the cries of Christian

mothers, terrified that their child might be sacrificed on the altar of Diana. The patron saint of Arelate halted the animal sacrifices, expunged images of Diana from the arena, and replaced them with Christian icons.

The arena at the very top of the rock of Arles abuts the fortress wall the Romans built there, part of which had to be removed to make way for the arena's construction. After it was decommissioned as a place of bloody spectacle, it became the refuge of ultimate defense, behind which the people of Arles were repeatedly forced to retreat, hunkering down, protected by the largely impenetrable walls of Roman stone. In one of the worst times, they built two hundred wooden houses and two chapels inside the ruins of the amphitheater and lived there, as in a village, with a minuscule church at my summit dedicated to St. Michael of the Climb. His church was honored as usual by being set up high, facing the setting sun. He protected the city from evil demons who swarmed at dusk. It wasn't until 1830 that the arena was finally cleared and returned to its original function: presenting an image of war, the spectacle of bloody battles between ferocious combat bulls and modern lions dressed in gold.

Combat bulls have an ancient history in Arles, pre-Roman even; later the town and its Camargue were the source of all the bulls used in the gladiator games. In Arles they were regularly part of the pregame ceremonies in the arena. They were invited to attack dummies scattered around the floor and encouraged to launch them magnificently into the air. The crowds in Arles loved to see the wild bulls, not cattle but aurochs, piqued into a rage before they came into the arena to fight one another or other animals—lions, wild boar, elephants similarly disposed. Aurochs are the wild origin of many forms of cattle. Their name comes from Old High German, which combined the prefix *ur*, meaning "original," "primal," "first," "earliest," and *ohsa*, for "ox." *Urhosa* became *auroch*. Before aurochs went extinct in Poland in the seventeenth century, they roamed the forests of Europe. The bulls were of an unimaginable size, six feet tall at the shoulder, as high as they were long, compared to four and a half feet for a large combat bull, which ordinarily might weigh as much as thirteen hundred pounds. Some aurochs weighed more than three thousand pounds. Compared with domestic cattle, they had slender legs, which indicates they were fast as well as strong, also intelligent like their descendants, and with murderous intentions when provoked and sensing danger. They were at the center of the cult of Mithras. Bulls still obsess the imagination and haunt the phantasms of people in Arles. They belong to its very soil. In *La Bête du Vaccarès*, Joseph d'Arbeau included a great story in Provençal about a *gardien*, a cowboy like himself, who hunts and falls in love with a mysterious half man, half bull lurking in the Camargue *[The Rock misreads. The beast is half man, half goat—a satyr or the god Pan.]* Aficionados over the course of a career watching bullfights generally transition from loving the torero to loving the toro. Because Augustus decorated his theater with the sculpted heads of bulls, Arlesians have known that behind the mask, underneath the horns, is a thinking being like us—a sort of Minotaur, a demigod.

St. Augustine in his *Confessions* tells of his virtuous young friend Alypus, who couldn't resist the intoxicating pleasure that the spectacle of blood procures: *et cruenta voluptate inebriabatur*. Dragged to the arena by friends, he swore he would not be tempted to view the spectacle, but when a clamor went up from the crowd, he opened his eyes. Augustine writes:

> For, as soon as he saw the blood, he imbibed with it a savage temper, and he did not turn away, but fixed his eyes on the bloody pastime, unwittingly drinking in the madness—delighted with the wicked contest and drunk with blood lust. He was now no longer the same man who came in but was one of the mob he had come in with, a true companion of those who had brought him thither. Why need I say more? He looked, he shouted, he was excited, and he took away with him the madness that would stimulate him to come again: not only with those who first enticed him, but even without them; indeed, dragging in others besides.[2]

Blood lust, the desire to kill or watch killing, has the power to overwhelm the moral restraints of the Christian disciple induced to watch by the compelling spectacle of flowing gore and the erotic madness it excites. Some Roman lovers of the spectacle in the arena say they attend principally to observe the precise instant when a fierce living being, human or animal, passes from life to death. These days, twice a year at the ferias, twenty thousand Arlesians gather to watch bulls bred to kill being killed, under the hot sun of Provence.

The blood of the bull was spilled by Mithras as he plunged the dagger into the heart of the bull, one knee on its back, his cape flying with stars, while the dog and the snake tried to drink its blood and the scorpion to sting its balls. Bull balls have forever been endowed with magical powers: even today they become the obsession of families that lose a matador. They cannot rest until they have eaten the balls of the bull that killed their brother and son.

The spilled blood of the sacrificial victim explains many things in Arles. Think of St. Genesius, who at first was a soldier, then became known for his proficiency at writing and was made secretary to the chief magistrate of the city. The patron saint of Arles was a scribe, literally a writer, what Plato calls a "logograph," one who wrote the words of others, more clearly, more beautifully than anyone else in the army. When the persecution of Christians was announced in his office, he is supposed to have been outraged by the injustice, refused to sign the death warrants ordered by Diocletian, to have thrown his tablets at the feet of the magistrate and fled. The young catechumen went looking for a priest to baptize him, but the bishop didn't trust him and assured him that martyrdom was as good as baptism in the eyes of Jesus. Condemned to death, he fled, swimming across the river to Trinquetaille, where he was arrested by soldiers and decapitated. Genesius wasn't yet a Christian, only on his way to renouncing his pagan beliefs before being accepted into the cult. His refusal, and his martyrdom on behalf of Christ, meant that he was baptized in his own blood: his life as a Christian began with his death as a Christian; his birth was simultaneous with his death—a great blessing, it was thought. His head was then transported back across the river to the left bank and buried in the old Roman cemetery of Alyscamps, outside the city walls. On each side of the double city of Arles, cult places arose to mark the martyrdom of its patron saint.

The blood of St. Genès flowed on the right side of the Rhône, and where it fell there sprouted a myrtle tree, whose black berries drank his spilled blood. The tree was so enthusiastically venerated by crowds of worshippers that the myrtle soon lost its leaves, then its branches, and had to be replaced by a column, later a church, Our Lady of the Column. Arles became known for centuries as a city protected by the blood and body of its martyr.

In the second quarter of the fifth century, St. Hilaire pronounced a sermon in honor of St. Genès that described the procession on August 25, the saint's day, which went from his place of martyrdom in Trinquetaille to the cemetery of Alyscamps. To do so, it had to cross the Rhône on the bridge of ships, which was still the only bridge across. The weight of the crowd on the bridge collapsed it, but the prayers that rose from the faithful elicited the protection of St. Genès, so no one's loss was deplored. The blood of St. Genès so powerfully protected the city of Arles on both sides of the Rhône for so long that it became legendary, and Arles was sometimes known as *urbs Genesii*.

St. Genès hasn't always been so protective of his city. Since his martyrdom, oceans of blood over the centuries have flooded the streets of Arles. In the third century, Roman Gaul was shaken by invasions of Gothic barbarians; the tribe of Alemani crossed the Rhine and soon stormed the walls of the city before burning most of it down, on both sides of the Rhône. Devastated and largely destroyed, the city was rebuilt in forty years, grander than ever, mainly by Emperor Constantine, who lived here in his palace and loved the city. I've been invaded and captured, sometimes briefly, sometimes for years, by Visigoths and Lombards, Catalans, Vikings and Normans, but the worst were the Sarrassins, those Berbers who had come through Spain conquering everything until they were finally stopped at Poitiers by Charles Martel, the father of Charlemagne, who chased them south to the coast. Even after being roundly repulsed, they continued to raid Provence, seized and occupied a region near Saint Tropez, and from there launched lightning forays on cities all around, pillaging, burning, raping, and selling their captives into slavery.

Vivien, the son of William of Orange, the lord of Provence, was killed and his army defeated at an epic battle in the Alyscamps cemetery. His heroic deeds were commemorated in a *chanson de geste*, "Aliscans," which paints the flower of Christian chivalry lying dead and dying in the necropolis, the sarcophagi overflowing with their fresh corpses. The Muslims took over the city. It's they who built the watchtowers on the arena, taught the people medicine, and generally enhanced the city, contrary to popular belief. They inhabited parts of Gallia for three hundred years and weren't finally expelled until the tenth century.

The necropolis of Alyscamps was already widely known in antiquity. Dante mentions it in the *Inferno*:

> *Si come ad Arli, ove Rodano stagna*
> *…fanno I supulcri tutt'il loco varo,*
> *Cosi facevan quivi d'ogne parte,*
> *Salvo che'l modo v'era più amoro.*

> Just as at Arles, where the Rhône slows,
> The sepulchers make the ground uneven,
> As they did here all around, only here [*in Hell*]
> the nature of it was more terrible.[3]

The name Alyscamps comes by way of Provençal from the Latin, *Elisii Campi*, Elysian Fields… or Champs Elysée. Roman cemeteries were always located outside the city walls. Built southeast of the city, along the Aurelian Way leading into Arles, Alyscamps spread over the centuries to become one of the biggest in Europe. In recent centuries, encroached upon by industry and development, the cemetery has been reduced to a fraction of its former size. For centuries, corpses were piled on corpses in the great sandstone sarcophagi that fill the cemetery in front of the Church of Saint-Honorat, one of the first archbishops of Arles.

Once the martyred head of St. Genès was buried in the Alyscamps, in 303, all the archbishops of Arles wanted to be buried there too—such was the prestige of the blood of martyrs. St. Trophime, one of the first and greatest bishops of Arles, started the tradition. It was said that Christ himself attended his funeral and left the imprint of his knee on a sarcophagus lid. Then came nobles, then the rich. People upstream as far as Lyon would attach a corpse to a skiff and send it down to Arles with money and a note attached asking for it to be buried in the Alyscamps. Today the museum is filled with the most intricately carved sandstone sarcophagi, commissioned by those with means.

Some from the fourth century are carved with both pagan and Christian motifs; one, for example, has carved on its lid Castor and Pollux guiding souls, while on the side panels, Christ is multiplying loaves and fishes. The intricate carvings on the sarcophagi were intended for the attention of the dead, not for the living—proof of which is that they were usually entombed below the pavement, invisible to view.

This was the decisive moment when Christianity overcame the pagan gods and began prohibiting their worship. The light of classical culture dimmed and went dark for ages, under the weight of fanaticism and superstition. The first, the real Renaissance occurred in the twelfth century, when the darkness was illuminated by the rediscovery of Greek philosophy and science, as they were transmitted through Hebrew and Arab texts. The so-called Renaissance of the fifteenth century was a paler incarnation of the radical rebirth that occurred in the twelfth century, when the mystification and obscurantism of Christian centuries were dispelled by the rediscovery in the West of Plato and Aristotle, with their tradition of logical argument and scientific observation. Statues on the facade of Saint-Trophime, the great twelfth-century Provençal cathedral in the central square of Arles, illustrate the fusion of classical and Christian motifs that produced the renaissance of the Romanesque. Next to Daniel, surrounded by the lions in their den, you have an adorable Hercules, of Greek legend, fighting the Nemean lion. Farther to the side, just below a monstrous figure of the Devil, with a long tail and a naked woman emerging from its genitals, parades a charming little centaur. There are no centaurs in the Gospels; Hercules in late antiquity was a demigod much beloved of emperors, whereas centaurs, like Chiron, the tutor of Achilles, were the teachers of mankind.

With that, the Rock grew silent, and I took it the session was over. I started to get up when the Rock stopped me in my tracks:

Chiron! I thought that might catch your attention. You wrote in 1986:

In Ptolemy's catalogue of the constellations, Chiron, the centaur, is represented as carrying a wolf in one hand and in the other a thyrsus. The emblem may be taken as a sign of the creature's double postulation, allegorized by Nietzsche as a figure for the aspiration of classical philology, linking a strange, demonic cruelty that betrays and disrupts all alliances with a sublime wisdom of the mysteries of generation and the double spiraling movement of time. The wolf in the centaur breaks the circle; the thyrsus initiates it.[4]

Don't you think I know that at the beginning of your career you wrote a thesis titled "Thyrsus: The Ironic Stance of Baudelaire's Poetry" and that what Nietzsche here calls classical philology describes exactly the aspiration of your cruel version of literary critical theory? I note for example "Oxymorons of Anxiety: or the Influence of Baba Ram Dass on Harold Bloom."[5]

A centaur: a wolf, a thyrsus—that's you, you wish.

Whoa! I was stunned. I felt eviscerated. The Rock knew more about me than I do. I crawled upstairs and did what I always do to calm myself: I went to the refrigerator.

Peri Tuché

The next day I took my place in the cellar with some trepidation. After a long while, the Rock began to speak:

Sorry if I alarmed you yesterday. But old Rocks can only tell the truth. Besides, I've gotten ahead of myself. We've only just come to the tragic fourth century, when everything changed for the worst and the fate of the world was turned away from the wisdom of *paideia* to what St. Paul, in "First Corinthians," calls, by litotes, the foolishness of Christ. What appears foolish to the pagan mind steeped in logic and science is to Paul a higher wisdom. All this explains why the world needs Favorinus more than ever, not just in Arles. Having been forgotten for a millennium and a half, he can teach you how to live without religion. Favorinus believed in the gods because they served to inspire so much literature. Poets invented marvelous myths about their doings, and those myths came to compose what we call Greek and Latin literature. The stories of the gods and heroes and the behaviors they illustrate served as well to reflect the values those people took to be exemplary. Favorinus knows the stories of every god and goddess, all the heroes and demigods as well. When he orates, he calls upon these stories to color his arguments, to persuade his listeners with their illustration when his philosophical categories fail him. In that he's like Plato, except he goes very fast, cites myths almost telegraphically, counting on his audience to remember the narratives. Prolixity, producing lots of examples and floods of words, was a virtue in sophists, who got paid to speak for hours.

Favorinus probably didn't believe in every god and goddess, but it was prudent under the empire to act as if he did. You might say he was almost a monotheist. He believed mainly in one god who created everything and ruled everywhere: Tuché, the goddess of chance or fortune. It is she who gives not only good fortune and bad, but even attributes and qualities at birth; it is she who gives wealth and fortune to the rich, and beautiful bodies to handsome men. It's she who exalts the humble and casts down the proud, who raises up kings and is accused when they fall. Even Alexander the Great, who triumphed over the grandest armies, was brought low by Tuché so to die on his couch, poisoned by his cupbearer. If you aspire to wisdom, not wealth, and wish only to live a frugal, virtuous life, then it's Tuché, Favorinus says, who made you a philosopher.

"Chance, or Tuché," he says, quoting Demosthenes, "is the greatest, or rather the only determining cause of everything." Tuché decides everything, from the choice of your genes to the fall of empires, and there is nothing you can do to make it serve your interest except . . . pray. You may think of yourself as especially worthy of the good luck you enjoy, but the thing about luck—it changes. One day you're up, the acrobat in the circus, brilliant in skin-white tights, flying like a god, the next you're a clown tripping over itself into a bucket of shit. Life is changing fortune, says Favorinus, nothing more than a carnival parade.

Favorinus was a contrarian, according to Aulus Gellius, his faithful stenographer: the philosopher cultivated in his speech arguments for and against things, and loved to produce persuasive orations in favor, for example, of old age, or of gladiators, whose bloody cruelty many condemned. On one inaugural occasion, he delivered a brilliant speech, "In Defense of the Baths," at a time when pagan moralists ever since Pythagoras and Christian ones like Tertullian were hostile to the public baths, considering them to be places of well-being and pleasure, hence full of watery demons. Favorinus doubtless wrote to please Hadrian as well. The emperor had built numerous baths around the empire and had the habit of publicly washing himself among the people.

Favorinus wrote to praise quartan fever, which is a variety of malaria: "According to Plato, a man affected by this illness enjoys, after his cure, a much more robust state of health than before." He wrote a text in favor of Thersites, the plebian soldier in Homer's *Iliad* (the only plebian who speaks among all the nobles), who defies King Agamemnon and proposes, after nine years

VI.1. Plaque for the lane named after Favorinus

camped before the walls of Troy, that they stop the war and return home already. He is slapped around, denounced, and ridiculed by Odysseus and the other nobles, who naturally want to continue the war. Marx, as well, was a great admirer of Thersites, this proletarian soldier who was seeking peace.

Aulus Gellus says that Favorinus "took great pleasure in these sorts of paradoxical subjects, persuaded that they were useful for keeping the mind alive, for familiarizing it with subtle arguments, and as a hedge against difficulties."[1] At the heart of every paradox is a seeming contradiction or absurdity that, under analysis, proves to be true. Contrarians like Favorinus defend the opposite, the double other of conventional wisdom. As a child of Arles, he must have imbibed the doubleness of Arles, *urbs dupleix*, pro and contra, right and left, with his mother's milk.

As the Rock of Arles, I am naturally biased, if I may say, in favor of any son (or daughter) of Arles, but I deeply believe that Favorinus was the greatest philosopher in the Roman Empire in the second century. As I've told you, he flourished during the period of what has been called the Second Sophistic, which alludes to the first great period of rhetoric six hundred years earlier, in the fifth and fourth centuries [BCE] in Athens, when certain Greek lecturers, writers, and teachers, who called themselves sophists, traveled about the Greek-speaking world giving instruction in a wide range of subjects in return for fees. They were among the greatest adversaries of Socrates, who was often deemed to be one of them.

Six hundred years later, in the first and second centuries, a renaissance of Hellenic oratory and Greek education captivated the Roman elites. In the Second Sophistic, figures like Favorinus could be orators as well as authentic philosophers. People today know little about him. Only three of his works have survived. There's the speech he gave, "To the Corinthians," when he returned there to discover that the city had removed his statue, which had been erected in his honor after an earlier visit. He also wrote *On Exile*, drawing on his experience during his five-year banishment to the island of Chios. I especially recommend his most important surviving work, his little book *Peri Tuché* (*On Fortune*). It's depressing that most of his strictly philosophical works have been lost. Only bits and fragments, fragments of fragments, of his work have been recorded and transmitted in the writing of other authors, pagan and Christian, in antiquity.

It's been said that Favorinus was the sort of radical thinker whose innovation consisted in taking traditional premises to their hyper-logical conclusion. To my mind, Favorinus was radical to the extent that he embraced notions like those of Jacques Derrida, France's greatest modern philosophical master. But as far as mastery goes, I've heard that Derrida was inclined to repeat the Zen koan by which Nietzsche directed his disciples: "Follow me by not following me."

Derrida, the most radical contemporary philosopher, knew nothing, of course, about Favorinus. But it's striking to see how their writings converge not only around common themes but also in the way they attended to the logic of arguments.

Like Favorinus, Derrida paid meticulously close attention, scrupulous and detailed, to the smallest differences of meaning. Both had a deep philosophical interest in etymology, the study of the origin of words intended to discover conceptual implications hidden or repressed in contemporary usage or meaning. They both insisted on calling things by their right name so as to preserve precise distinctions. As Favorinus affirmed, "Since for Roman citizens speaking Latin, it is no less disgraceful not to designate a thing by its proper noun than it is not to call a man by his own name."[2]

They were both amazingly prolific writers on a great variety of subjects. Derrida wrote more than eighty books. Favorinus had the ambition to write as many books as his friend Plutarch, "an infinite number," his contemporaries thought—more exactly, 277. Plutarch's son estimated that Favorinus had written 210.

Both philosophers were deeply interested in the law. Derrida wrote a fat book about law and philosophy. Favorinus, according to Aulus Gellus, used to consult with the greatest jurists in Rome over details of the first Roman system of laws, the twelve tables written in 551 [*BCE*].

They were both attentive readers of literature. Derrida wrote on Mallarmé and Ponge, two of the greatest, most difficult French poets, and his masterpiece, *Glas*, concerns Jean Genet (and Hegel). Many consider Genet to be the greatest writer of prose in French in the twentieth century. Only Derrida could find a way to persuasively link the work of a convict hustler thief to Hegel's systematic philosophy and make it seem not only plausible but unavoidable.

Favorinus used to demonstrate the difference between Pindar's Greek poetry and the Latin poetry of Virgil by quoting passages where the two poets describe the identical eruption of Mount Etna. He showed in detail why the Greek poet's language is more precise and coherent, more vivid and poetically powerful. It confirmed the prejudice of Favorinus, who thought that the Greek language, like all things Greek, was more beautiful than Latin. (The Romans, he allowed, were better at law.)

Favorinus needs only one line—*Scrattae, scrupedae, strictivillae, sordidae* [*Despicable sluts, crippled, shriveled, shabby*]—from a lost play to recognize with certainty the style of Plautus, the great Latin comic playwright.

Favorinus wrote a discourse against tyranny; Derrida wrote a book on the democracy to come. He wrote a piece, "On Plato's Pharmacy"; Favorinus wrote "Plato and His Ideas." He wrote a book, *On Socrates and the Art of Love*. Derrida, in *The Post Card: From Socrates to Freud and Beyond*, envelops Socrates philosophically in the story of an affair told through a selection of postcards between lovers.

Finally, they were both cosmopolitan: Derrida wrote a little book addressed to "Cosmopolitans of Every Country," in which he calls for the renewal of international law, for which he "longs." Favorinus was the incarnation of the universality of the Roman Empire. You might even say the Romans invented the political idea of the universal: the equality of a multiplicity of autonomously governed cites within an overarching authoritarian state. Favorinus promoted a sort of Panhellenism that sought to bring the benefits of Greek language and culture to Romans as well as to "barbarians," to all the different cities and cultures that Favorinus visited in his ceaseless professional travels orating and teaching around the empire—around Europe, Asia, and the Middle East. Hellenism implied the greatest opening and tolerance toward all the different forms of civil society that existed in the empire.

Despite—or rather because of—being Celt, he felt more strongly the power of Greek-Roman culture to raise up a barbarian like him as a model of civilization: a eunuch, no less, a philosopher with no beard. His encyclopedic learning, his divine memory, his fluency in three languages, his supreme mastery of the Greek language, his charm and persuasiveness, his wicked wit imposed him on the public and attracted the friendship of the emperor despite his origins and his intersexuality. He was a warrior in the war with burgeoning Christianity; paganism was a unifying force in the empire, supported by the state, serving to counter the centrifugal appeal of the spreading Christian cult. He defended polytheism, with its myths and legends, whose many gods were not objects of transcendent feelings but rather emblems of personal conflicts and paradigms of virtue, composing a kind of early psychology. In his system the only god that finally mattered, in a world of constant change, was Tuché. Chance, fortune—the throw of the dice—rule everything.

It seemed to Favorinus that he might have been sent by the gods, as if by design, among the Hellenes, to provide proof to the natives of Greece that it mattered little to have been born or to have received one's education there to acquire fame and renown. Favorinus sees in himself the champion of a civilizing, universal mission that arose from an ideal that aimed to unify the people of the empire, and ultimately the world. He represented what the Greeks called *paideia*, mental and physical training aimed at producing a harmonious human being with access to the accumulation of knowledge and learning that composed the totality of what humans could rationally think and know.

The great Greek legislator Solon was asked how to raise an Athenian in the virtues of paideia. Here's what he is supposed by Lianus to have said:

Their early breeding, we leave to their mothers, nurses, and tutors, who are to rear them in the elements of a liberal education. But as soon as they attain to a knowledge of good and evil, when reverence and shame and fear and ambition spring up to them, when their bodies begin to set and strengthen and be equal to toil, then we take them over, and appoint them both a course of mental instruction and discipline, and one of bodily endurance. We are not satisfied with mere spontaneous development either for body or soul; we think that the addition of systematic teaching will improve the gifted and reform the inferior.

We first kindle their minds with music and arithmetic, teach them to write and to read with expression. Then, as they get on, we versify, for the better impressing their memories, the sayings of wise men, the deeds of old time, or moral tales. And as they hear of worship won and works that live in song, they yearn ever more, and are fired to emulation, that they, too, may be sung and marveled at by them that come after and have their Hesiod and their Homer. And when they attain their civil rights, and it is time for them to take their share in governing, we regulate their sentiments partly by teaching them the laws of the land. . . . We teach them to speak with propriety, act with justice, content themselves with political equality, eschew evil, pursue good, and abstain from violence; sophists and philosophers are the names by which these teachers are known.[3]

It was their shared view of the superiority of things Greeks that led Favorinus to become—for a while—an intimate friend of Hadrian, until the moment he aroused his anger and was sent into exile. Among other things, Favorinus had refused the honor of becoming an archpriest in the temple of Augustus in Arles. He probably resisted the idea of giving up his fabulous life in Rome for a life, however prestigious, in the colonies. Perhaps, too, he didn't like the idea of having to perform animal sacrifices, having become a vegetarian like his master Empedocles.

Besides the similarity of their choice of subjects, Favorinus practiced a form of radical skepticism that Derrida might have considered a deconstruction of the philosophical arguments that at that time dominated debates between different schools of philosophy and their teachers. Like deconstruction, his skepticism was not a nihilism that simply negated previous arguments but sought to reformulate old oppositions into new configurations. Favorinus, who wrote a work titled "Ten Pyrrhonien Tropes," was first identified with the radical skepticism of the New Academy, the one into which the former Academy of Plato had been transformed. The school of Academicians understood that because nothing could be understood, nothing therefore could be decided to be true. The school of Pyrrhoniens, yet more radically skeptical, refused even to subscribe to the truth of that proposition, because for them, nothing is true—not even the assertion that the truth can't be determined. Favorinus had understood better than others that the radical skepticism of the Academy led directly to the danger of what the Greeks called *apraxis*—the inability to act, to do anything at all because nothing could be decided. That is why Favorinus adopted a theoretical position that goes something like this:

If, as Pyrrhonien skeptics say, nothing is true, then the archi-skeptical position, which says one can't decide anything as to its truth, is not true either. So negating the skeptical negation in the name of an even more radical skepticism allows Favorinus to pass judgments on lots of different subjects on the basis, the Rock thinks, not of concepts, of conceptual criteria, but of aesthetic and scientific judgments. It's what allowed him to comment upon a vast number of subjects in ways that seemed truthful and wise to his disciples, without his having conceptual criteria by which to distinguish absolutely what the Greeks called *doxa*, "opinion," from *aletheia*, "truth."

Favorinus is radical not only by virtue of the topics he treats, the myths he demystifies, the conventional wisdom he overturns, but also the fact that, like Derrida, he aimed to push the boundaries of what it's possible to think. It entailed discovering new ways to think about the coherence of terms that seem, in the light of conventional logic, to be contradictory. Consider the logic of the supplement that Derrida explains in his first great book, *Of Grammatology*. A supplement, he says, may be a *mere* supplement, the addition of something that doesn't alter the thing itself, merely an external, extrinsic, inessential accessory that changes nothing in the thing that is already complete in itself. Because the supplement adds nothing essential, because it is external to the thing itself—doesn't belong to it inherently—it may be a dangerous addition, corrupting what it comes upon.

At other times the supplement is what is required for a deficient nature to be completed, to be fulfilled. The supplement fulfills the thing to which it is added, allowing it to become fully what it is. In Rousseau, as Derrida demonstrated, the nature of the child needs to be supplemented by education because of what it naturally lacks. But the supplement by adding something external and not natural is therefore potentially destructive. It must be administered so as to deform as little as possible the child's natural impulses. A supplement may therefore be, at the same time, depending on one's perspective, either a mere supplement adding nothing essential or the key piece whose addition allows it to be fully what it is, without which the thing is not complete. The single term fuses two essentially opposite connotations of the supplement. It is both what is most exterior, inessential, and what is most essential, that without which the thing is not what it is.

Derrida demonstrates how Rousseau tries to think contradictory notions simultaneously. The supplement of education is both essential to the child's completion and, by virtue of being extrinsic, nonnatural, is potentially dangerous. Derrida shows how Rousseau and Lévi-Strauss are constantly hesitating between these two uses.

Favorinus found the same solution to the logic of the supplement in his encounter with a Stoic and a Peripatetic philosopher who argued different sides of an ethical question: does virtue suffice to produce happiness?

The Stoic philosopher believes that for a life to be unhappy, it is enough to be wicked, and because virtue is the opposite of wickedness, it follows, by the logic of contraries, that it is enough to be virtuous to have a happy life.

No! says the Peripatetic philosopher. It is true that wickedness and vicious thoughts are enough to make life wretched, but virtue alone is by no means enough to make a happy life. Happiness requires more of other things: good health, property, a good reputation, a fair appearance, some wealth. At that, the Stoic philosopher loudly protests: if you agree that there's no happiness without virtue, how can you deny that virtue by itself is enough to make a happy life? You honor virtue when it's missing (without it there can be no happiness); you malign it when it's present (its presence is not enough in order to be happy).

The Peripatician wittily countered: "Tell me whether you think that an amphora [*six gallons*] of wine from which a conge [*six pints*] has been taken is still an amphora of wine."

"By no means," replied the Stoic, "can that be called an amphora of wine."

Whereupon the Peripatician replied: "Then it will have to be said that one conge makes an amphora, since, when that one is lacking, it is not an amphora of wine, but when it is added, it makes an amphora. Whereas, if it is absurd to say that a single conge will make an amphora, it is similarly absurd to say that virtue alone will make a happy life, even though, when virtue is absent, there can never be a happy life."

Favorinus, turning to the Peripatician, protests: "This ought to be seen rather as a charming fallacy, a sort of trick, rather than an honest or plausible argument. For when a conge is lacking, it indeed makes the amphora not to be a full measure. When it is added, and put in, it alone does not make the amphora, it supplements it [*supplet*—i.e., fills it up, makes it complete]. Virtue, however, as the Stoics say, is neither an addition nor a supplement, but it alone is equivalent to [*instar est*] a happy life, and therefore it alone makes a happy life when it is present."[4]

Favorinus makes a Derridean argument by demonstrating that there is no difference between virtue and happiness because virtue is not other than, exterior to, happiness, any more than speech is radically other than writing, dependent as it is on qualities associated with writing—for example, spacing, repetition. Virtue is not a thing added, a supplement [*non accessio, neque supplementum*], but itself alone is equivalent to [*instar est*] a happy life and therefore alone by itself [*sola ipsa*], when it's present, makes a happy life.

Although I know Derrida never read Favorinus, it sometimes feels, uncannily, as if Favorinus had read Derrida.

A hundred years after it was laid waste by Roman armies, Corinth was refounded as a Roman colony by Julius Caesar, shortly before his assassination. Corinth had a large, mixed, tolerant population of Greeks and Jews and Christians, and by the time Favorinus first went there, around 130, it had become the richest, most powerful city in Greece. His orating created an enormous sensation. On an isthmus in the Aegean, where everyone spoke Greek, Corinthians had never heard anyone speak it like Favorinus, with such marvelous abundance of language, full of colorful expressions in long periodic sentences, which enchanted listeners with their Attic rhythms. The impression of someone otherworldly was enhanced by the extraordinary elegance and refinement of his gestures, the complex modulations of his voice that sometimes became a form of singing. But the matter, no less than the manner, of his speech was equally preternatural, because, as I've said, it seemed as if he knew everything that could be learned in the second century. He argued abstruse questions of philology with the greatest grammarians, citing myriad examples on the spot from his divine memory of Greek and Latin history and literature. He visited sick friends and consulted the doctors because he had read all their books of medicine and more. With the greatest jurisconsults he discussed in detail the origins of Roman law.

So impressed were the Corinthians by his art, his genius, and his learning that on his second visit they tried to persuade him to stay and become their official orator and philosopher, publicist, and defender of the city. When he declined, in his stead they erected a bronze statue in his honor (Corinthian bronze was famous in antiquity) and installed it at the entrance to the Library of Corinth so that students might be inspired by his example.

Before his third visit to Corinth, Favorinus had quarreled with the emperor, who might have killed him but instead softly exiled him to the island of Chios in the Adriatic, famous for its wine and women. The minute Hadrian dies, Favorinus flies home to Rome, where he has a house and a great library, many friends and pupils who follow him around, admiringly. When he next returns to Corinth, he discovers that the rulers of the colony had caused his statue, as well as the pedestal on which they had placed him, to disappear. Indignant at the injustice of it, done with no explanation, he addresses the city through the voice of his statue, who undertakes to mount a defense of Favorinus— he being too modest to speak directly on his own behalf. It was one of the conventions of public oratory that one didn't boast or praise oneself. If he must congratulate himself, the orator should give the impression that he is constrained by circumstances very much against his will. Envy is the major obstacle to the success of self-praise. One avoids envy by making the discourse indirect, hiding the ego of the orator by putting the praise in the mouth of another. In his discourse to the Corinthians, it's not he but his statue who is heard speaking magnificently in his defense. In the same way, if someone does publish this auto-orography, few readers will believe that these are the words of a rock. They'll think it's a rhetorical conceit that lets the author speak in praise or blame of things that might offend, by attributing the words to an impersonal, inorganic Other.

If you are one of those skeptical readers, I must insist that I am quite incapable of speaking about Arles at such length and in such intimate detail. But why should you believe me?

Favorinus knew from hearing me, the Rock of Arles, whispering to him all those years, that bronze, like stone, can speak to those who can hear. You remember, too, that I said that statues in antiquity were not intended merely to represent the gods and heroes within but rather to make them visible. Someone chose to make his statue vanish, to the detriment of Corinthians—whose ancestors more than any others had cultivated *dikaiosunei*, justice, said the statue. It was they, after all, who had freed Athens from tyranny, overturned tyrants, and installed democracy.

Finding the statue gone, Favorinus reminds the Corinthians, in his angry speech, that they dishonor the honor they paid him by taking down his statue. Not self-interested, as it might appear, his anger is aroused in defense of the values and the wisdom that it was the intention of the city to celebrate in the first place by honoring him with a statue. Such a prize was awarded not even to Arion, Corinth's most famous poet, he who invented the dithyramb, the poetic meter in which Greek tragedy is declaimed. Favorinus, before going on, pauses to digress to remind his listeners of the legendary success of Arion and his dubious reward at the hands of his fellow Corinthians.

Sailing back to Corinth after earning great sums for his singing, Arion was seized by the sailors on his ship, greedy for his money and indifferent to his fame. As he was about to be thrown overboard, he asked for the right, like a swan, to embark his soul on a ship of song. He began to sing; there was calm and silence on the ocean. Dolphins, hearing the song, surrounded the ship. When he had finished, the sailors weren't softened, so Arion jumped into the sea. At that moment, a dolphin rose up and transported him to Corinth, dressed as he was in his performance robes, ahead of the wicked sailors. When they arrived, their crime was revealed, and they were put to death. However, Arion was obliged by the meanness of Corinth to erect a statue of himself for himself, not a very big one, seated on his benefactor, a dolphin. The story of Arion is intended to remind his audience that Favorinus, by his statue, was more highly honored than even their greatest artist and native son. It was also a veiled threat against those who had removed his statue, who, having once enjoyed his gifts, like the sailors, turned on him and now were dishonored by dishonoring him in his statue. They deserved to be discovered and punished.

Favorinus mocks the generosity of Corinth toward its greatest artists but, in his own case, is dismayed that the city had such little respect, not for him in person, but for the tribute they had paid him, for the principles of paideia he represented so magnificently and that they had wished to transmit to their students.

There are many reasons, he says, to erect a statue. But it's not at all the same thing to make the decision to tear it down. Why? Because each of your offerings, whether beautiful or ugly, from the moment it is made, acquires a sacred character, becomes a token of the city's honor, and the city must protect it as an offering. In the case of a statue, the weight of the authority at the time the statue was erected should be respected. Otherwise, people might rightly wonder about the ephemeral time of your honors and the eternal character of your dishonors. Your statues are softer than wax that melts away, he said angrily.

The statue of Favorinus answers those Corinthians who say that his statue was removed to please Hadrian, who exiled him. To the contrary, the statue argues that removing him is misguided, for leaving it in place would be much more in line with values Hadrian was keen to promote. If the Corinthians honor me, the orator, they would be honoring even more the emperor, who cares only to appear to be, in everything, like Favorinus himself, a Hellene.

In speaking to the Corinthian public, Favorinus had to know that it was composed of Christians, as well as Jews, and others of Eastern origin.

The Corinthian Church had been living in peace with pagans for over a century. Christians there were entertained by nonbelievers in their homes, and they took meals in the annexed meeting rooms of the temples. Christian community gatherings were open to everyone. By the time Favorinus arrived in Corinth, near the beginning of the second century, Christianity was just beginning to experience the explosive growth that would lead to its triumph in the fourth century. The Christian war on paganism took off at the same time in the writings of Tertullian, the first great Christian theologian, the first to announce what became the orthodox Nicene doctrine of *homoousios*, the illogical Trinitarian argument that Father Son and Holy Ghost were all three of the same substance, neither one secondary nor subordinate to the others. Christians believed it on faith, I guess, because it was absurd. *Credo quia absurdum*, as Tertullian is supposed to have said.

Tertullian waged war against the pagan gods in the most violent terms. In his *Defense of Christianity*, he condemns them to their own Hell. Of them he says:

> They certainly didn't make the world, or anything that is in it. Nor do the whoring, raping, murderous crew you describe as gods deserve anything more than imprisonment in Tartarus, since that is where you would assign any man who behaved like that. If they don't deserve that, why do you condemn in your courts men who do the same sorts of things? You allow the public theaters to display your gods as entertainment, played by the shameful wretches you have as actors. You allow the temples to act as brothels, and priests as panders. Even the temple-robbers are always of your faith! So, what do we worship instead? We worship Truth.[5]

That is, Jesus Christ.

St. Paul, on the eve of his third visit to Corinth *[in 57 CE]*, found he had lost the trust and admiration of the important community of Christians who, like the admirers of Favorinus, had once welcomed him warmly. They now preferred Apollos, another disciple, to attend to their affairs. Paul had tried once before to win back their favor. Like Favorinus, he mounted a defense of his actions and his good name against those who had questioned his integrity and holiness. Paul was aware that he wasn't much of an orator, without the bodily presence of a great speaker or the rhetorical conventions that were taught in the schools, but his message, unlike that of Favorinus, was radically simple. Whereas Favorinus brought to his orations the whole wealth of his extraordinary learning as well as a skeptical philosophical mind, trained in logic and argumentation, Paul knows only one thing.

In his first letter to the Corinthians he writes: "And I, brethren, when I came to you, came not with excellency of speech or of wisdom, declaring unto you the testimony of God. For I determined not to know anything among you, save Jesus Christ and Him crucified. If any man among you seemeth to be wise in this world, let him become a fool, that he may be wise. For the wisdom of this world is foolishness."[6]

Paul tells philosophers that their wisdom is foolishness, and what they take to be foolish, a god dying on a cross like a thief, is wisdom, the sole and only truth there is, whereas Favorinus, addressing the Corinthians, preached the way to a harmonious life through the arduous path of acquiring the wisdom of paideia, the whole curriculum of physical training and intellectual instruction that had been accumulated in schools and preserved in books over a thousand years of Hellenistic civilization. All that is dismissed by Paul, who turns the page of philosophy with a stroke and insults the accomplishments of Greek thought and science with a turn of phrase. Nothing is worth knowing "save Jesus Christ and Him crucified." Whereas the education and training of paideia requires a long, laborious, no doubt expensive education, access to the only wisdom that mattered, the truth of Jesus Christ, was acquired instantaneously and at no cost. Paul had even canceled the Jewish requirement of circumcision.

Cosmopolitan salesmen for their conflicting ideologies, Paul and Favorinus were remarkably suited for their role in the empire: they both were trilingual. Whereas Favorinus spoke Celtic, Greek, and Latin, Paul spoke Hebrew, Latin, and Greek. His first audience was Hellenized Jews who all spoke and prayed in Greek in the synagogue. Christianity was born at the same time as the Roman Empire; both assumed a universal mission, to unite all peoples and all tongues under a single law. As some have said, the Roman peace, *Pax Romana*, was the nurse at the cradle of the religion of St. Paul of Tarsus and oversaw its growth. And among the many Christian sects that flourished between the first and fourth centuries, it is the specific group known as proto-Catholics that eventually triumphed over the others. By its universal character and its hierarchical organization modeled on the empire, with a pope for emperor, it was perfectly suited to become the state religion of a strongly centralized, ecumenical state.

By the Edict of Milan in 313, Constantine I declared Christianity to be an *airesis*, a philosophical choice, a doctrine among others benefiting from the freedom of being an authorized cult, a *religio licita*. This act of religious tolerance has been taken by Christian writers to mark the conversion of the empire to Christianity as the state religion. That would have to wait a hundred years. Constantine couldn't have anticipated the violence this act of tolerance would unleash and the controversies it would stir in the Christian world. Constantine worked to diminish conflicts within Christianity and at the same time showered it with privileges and benefits. The result was that people rushed to become priests to escape the burdens imposed on ordinary citizens and to enjoy the monetary and political advantages bestowed on this new professional class, with its growing demands.

Paul makes no secret of his eagerness to appear to become Jew or pagan, Roman or barbarian, freeman or slave, whatever guise was necessary to better persuade and convert the cosmopolitan audience of the empire. Favorinus similarly promotes his credentials to speak to the diversity of the empire, as if the gods had endowed him especially with the capacity to spread the blessings of paideia. It seems to him that he was made for this mission. To the Hellenes of Greece, he was proof of the fact that to be a master of Greek, to be among the greatest of all, one did not need to have been born in Greece or educated there. Any indigenous person who embraces paideia can aspire to acquire renown in Greek, the language of oratory in the second century. Just look at him, a barbarian eunuch.

It took four hundred years for superstition to triumph over science and philosophy. Just imagine what we might have become in the West if the wisdom of Favorinus, called foolish by Paul, had triumphed over the foolishness of Paul that he calls wisdom. For fifteen hundred years or more his church has pressed its deadening foolishness on the shoulders of humanity. The West has resisted its leaden oppression only during those periods when it has found inspiration from a return to the Hellenistic wisdom of Greece and Rome.

The Rock's view is that Christianity was a mistaken path taken by the Western world when it turned from promoting the value of this life to imagining a fiction of the next. The Church at last has all but collapsed under the weight of its irrelevance and corruption. The Arles of Favorinus offers another path. We are in one of those periods, like that of the second century, when old civic religions no longer command belief. There were official rites that had become sacred for maintaining the claims of the state. Christianity was one of many cults, both religious and secular—philosophical—that were competing for the allegiance of the people. You call them religions, as if you understand how that word is supposed to comprise many very different social practices, not to mention theological notions. The moment when the bishops began imposing their "religion" on the pagan, Jewish, Persian, Egyptian, Greek, and Roman "religions" can be traced to the year 313. That was the moment when the archbishop of Arles, the most powerful bishop outside Rome, persuaded

Emperor Constantine to call for a council of bishops in Arles, the first such Christian council under the auspices of imperial power. On that fateful day, the intolerant vision of St. Paul allied itself to political power, and within a century Christianity had eliminated other religious rites and practices. It used to be said, "The Roman Empire excludes from its tolerance only the intolerant." Think how different life would be if the tolerant vision of Favorinus had impressed itself on the emperor instead.

You are living at a moment like that of Favorinus, when the old gods are no longer believed and new gods have not yet been born. Perhaps you are at the birth of a world with no gods. Morality and faith would need to be redirected in ways that you've only just begun to glimpse. You need to turn away from faith in heaven in order, trembling, as in an aftershock, to promote faith in this life and the future of humanity. If it destroys itself, I'll be lonely and much less amused.

The Rock emitted what I took to be a laugh that rattled my wine bottles, and silence resumed.

Felix Carcar

The next day, I barely had time to sit down before the Rock resumed the story of the Christianization of Gaul:

Arles in the second century was the hub of the vast network of Roman roads that made it possible to move an ever-increasing number of travelers—troops and merchants, officials and traders, even tourists could take to the highways. The roads brought lamb from Britain and lumber from Russia, marble from Greece and dried fruit from Syria, and—most important of all—grain from the wheat-growing regions of North Africa. Arles was a crossroads of all this coming and going, doing plenty of business moving product up and down the Rhône and trading the bounty of its vast agriculture production.

Favorinus died in 161, just as Marcus Aurelius, the Stoic philosopher and adopted son of his predecessor, Antoninus Pius, became emperor. Arles was at the height of its prosperity and influence in the empire. Christians were a still small but growing sect among the myriad cults that prospered in Rome. Two hundred and thirty years later, in 389, the edict of Emperor Theodosius I made Christianity the state religion, and pagans who refused to cease their idolatrous worship—blood sacrifices, ritual prayer, and superstitious magic—were executed. With Theodosius, tolerance died. The Roman Empire had been intolerant only of the intolerant. In killing paganism, the Church killed tolerance. Now that churches are dying everywhere, tolerance may revive, even flourish. It may take another century if the world survives.

Marcus Aurelius was followed in the third century mostly by generals, many weak and cruel, beginning with his gladiator son Commodus, perhaps the craziest of all.

Or maybe not. A little later in the third century there was Elagabalus. He acquired his name from the eponymous Syrian sun god known as Heliogabalus, a solar deity, initially venerated in his mother's town of Emesa. Elagabalus declared Heliogabalus to be the chief god of the Roman pantheon, above even Jupiter, and renamed him Sol Invictus. Elagabalus is a Latinized version of the Syrian Ilāh hag-Gabal, which derives from *Ilah* (a Semitic word for "god") and *gabal* ("mountain" in Arabic), which produces "the God of the Mountain," the Emesene manifestation of the deity. Elagabalus forced senators to watch while he danced around the altar of El-Gabal, on which the god was manifest in the form of a conical meteorite—an avatar of the god on Earth. In case you're wondering about the Rock of Arles, as you may have guessed, yours truly (like El-Gabal) is a mountain god, the mountain manifestation of the god that inhabits me, *le Rocher d'Arles*, on which this city was founded. One day the world will know my story and come dance on my sides. When you've been around as long as I have and seen so much, you know—as Favorinus taught—that anything that can happen will happen. Sometimes, not in time.

Since the reign of Septimus Severus early in the third century, sun worship had become increasingly popular throughout the empire, as monotheism overcame the riot of multiple competing gods among the elites. Elagabalus had seen this as an opportunity to set up his god, El-Gabal, as the chief deity of the Roman pantheon. As a sign of the union between the two religions, Elagabalus gave Astarte, Minerva, Urania, or some combination of the three to El-Gabal as a wife. Later, the boy emperor had a temple built, the Elagabalium, on the Palatine Hill in Rome, of which he was the high priest. It was the center of a controversial new religious cult dedicated to Sol Invictus. I've heard rumors that children of rich and noble families were scooped up and brought to be sacrificed in the temple. The religious excesses of Elagabalus's reign eventually contributed to his demise.

At the summer solstice, there was a great festival devoted to El-Gabal; it was popular with the masses because food was widely distributed. During this festival, Elagabalus placed El-Gabal on a bejeweled chariot that he paraded through the city, throwing gifts into the Roman crowds. Then, climbing to the top of the high towers he had erected, he threw down cups of gold and silver, clothing, and every kind of cloth to the mob below. The most sacred relics of the Roman religion were brought from other shrines to the Elagabalium, the great temple of the god—even the fire of Vesta. The deity of Elagabalus was "also called Jupiter and Sol" (*fuit autem Heliogabali vel Iovis vel Solis*), and all the other Roman gods were ranged under him.

In the Phoenician mythology, one of the sons of Uranus was named Baetylus, which comes from the Semitic *Bet El* ("House of God"), the etymon of the technical word for a meteorite or other sacred stone that is supposed to be endowed with spirit. Since antiquity, meteorites have been worshipped, taken as bits of epiphany, appearances in the densest, material form of the godhead. St. Augustine in the fifth century was still having to denounce the worship of *baetyls* in North Africa long after Christianity had been officially adopted. The ancient Greeks worshipped the Omphalos, the stone thrown down by Zeus to mark the center, the navel of the Earth. It was wrapped in wool, anointed every day, and kept in a holy of holies at Delphi protected by the god Apollo. Gaia, the mother of Zeus, had tricked her husband, Cronos, who feared his children, by feeding it to him wrapped in swaddling clothes.

In Rome there was the stone effigy of Cybele, called Mater Idaea Deum, that had been ceremoniously brought from Pessinus in Asia Minor in 204 BCE. Think of another great holy stone, the Black Stone, in the *kaabah* in Mecca, which was worshipped by pre-Islamic polytheists. All that's left of the original holy meteorite, which fell in the Garden of Eden, are seven small pieces of the original bactyl that have been cemented together. In the tenth century, Qarmations from Eastern Arabia had attacked Mecca and carried off the black stone. They crushed it before returning it to Mecca for a rich ransom. Later the stones were fixed into a labial silver frame and attached to the eastern wall of the kaabah, where pilgrims crowd to kiss it as they circle around seven times.

Elagabalus was elevated to the imperial throne when he was barely fourteen years old by the Gallic Third Legion under the powerful influence of his grandmother, the brilliant, monstrous Julia Maesa. He was married, it's said, at least five times and lavished extravagant favors on his favorite husbands. He used to depilate his entire body and appear in court dressed (or undressed) as Venus. Once when the well-endowed Aurelius Zoticus addressed the emperor as "my lord," Elagabalus responded, "Don't call me lord, I am a lady." He advanced to high honors men noted for the size of their genitals. At times, he turned the imperial palace into a male brothel, in which he used to prostitute himself. It's said he asked his physicians to give him the equivalent of a vagina by means of a surgical incision. People have been transgendered in their unconscious mind long before it was ever actually possible.

He carried on like that until the day his own Praetorian Guard, enraged by his debauchery, extravagant perversity, piggishness, and arrogance—on the orders of the same grandmother who had put him on the imperial throne—killed him and contemptuously threw his body in the Tiber. He was said by some to be one of the filthiest monsters and most detestable tyrants that Rome ever produced. He reigned for only three years, nine months, and four days. They also murdered his mother, Julia Soaemias. Afterward, always happy to be helpful, Julia Maesa, after having lovingly arranged for her grandson to be killed, had him replaced by his cousin Severus Alexander. Elagabalus's religious edicts were reversed, and the statues that had been moved to the Elagabalium were restored to their original shrines.

Severus Alexander's reign of thirteen years was peaceful, prosperous, and the longest in seventy-five years. He worshiped in his private chapel not only Orpheus and Apollonius of Tyre, but also Abraham and Jesus Christ. While campaigning against the Germanic tribes, he attempted to buy peace with them using bribes and diplomacy. This besmirched the honor of some in the army, who conspired to assassinate and replace him.

It was while Severus Alexander was meeting in an open tent with angry troops, who compared him to his cousin Elagabalus (whose assassination had led to his reign), that a German servant entered and called for his death on the spot. In an instant a swarm of troops joined the attack against the emperor and his attendants. A few minutes later, he was dead; his mother, Julia Mamaea, who was in the same tent, met the same fate and died at the hands of the same assassins. His murder is considered the event that inaugurated fifty years of chaos known as the Crisis of the Third Century, when the empire nearly collapsed under intense pressure from Germanic tribes invading and migrating across the Rhine. Money became scarce and unreliable. Plagues decimated cities and the countryside. Commerce was drastically curtailed. Peasant rebellions and civil wars raged among the twenty-six claimants to the imperial throne, mostly usurping generals. The pagan historian Zosimos wrote that in the middle of the third century, the empire was "without a rudder, drifting from neglect."[1]

It was during this period of chaos and violence that Arles was invaded by the army of a German king with the charming name of Chrocus. The harbinger of spring was his name; no one seems to know why. He came with his hordes of

Gothic fighters across the border, pillaging and ravishing as they went. Chrocus is said to have been immensely arrogant. Having committed several crimes on the advice of his mother, he assembled the tribes of the Allemani, made himself king of the confederation, and led his troops across the Rhine into the center of Gaul, where he burned and pillaged temples, devastated cities and countryside alike with massacres and executions. Near Clermont-Ferrand, his rabble burned down the most beautiful Roman building in Gaul, the great pagan temple dedicated to Mercury, called by the Celtic inhabitants, in Gaulish, Vasso Galate. It was all in marble with double walls, thirty feet thick, brilliantly decorated with mosaics; its pavement was of marble, and the vast roof was of lead. Only part of a wall survives. It was probably the greatest and most magnificent example of Gallo-Roman architecture in all of Europe.

In 260, after several tries, Chrocus attacked Arles, which was totally unprepared after centuries of Roman peace. He all but burned it to the ground—on both sides of the Rhône. It put an end to the city's brilliant success and great prospects. From that point on it never fully recovered its former imperial glory, except in memory.

The Roman emperor finally mounted an army to defend the empire. A brave Roman centurion named Marius led a raid that captured Chrocus near Arles. They submitted him to various tortures, put him in chains, and paraded him around Gaul to witness the destruction he had left in his wake. They finally put him to the death he deserved at the point of a sword. For the Romans, anything that once was Roman was Roman forever.

Emperor Decius, in the exact middle of the third century, was the first to issue a systematic, empire-wide imperial edict against nonstate religions. Until then, persecution was a local affair that fell to pagan governors for whom being Christian was a crime. The edict of Decius in 249 was not particularly directed at Christians. He ordered all, except Jews (whose long tradition tabooed tasting blood), to practice animal sacrifices to the gods of the Roman people. The edict was also directed against Pythagoreans, Platonists, Hermetists, and other vegetarian cults and philosophies whose doctrines were opposed to bloody sacrifices. For Decius, as for subsequent emperors, only the piety of all the inhabitants of the empire could save it from the disasters that were befalling it: *Pax Deorum*, the peace of the gods, the unity of faith in the empire and the empire's gods was required of all its citizens. Though often mistaken by Christian apologists for the first systematic persecution of Christians, in fact his edict laid the basis for the later unification of the Christian religion and the Roman state by Constantine and his successors.

Once the sacrifices were accomplished, local commissioners had to certify that everyone who was obliged to sacrifice had complied; then they issued a certificate signed and attested, a so-called *libellus*, saying, "We have performed our libation, made sacrifices and tasted the sacred victim." Those who resisted or were caught out were brought to trial and put in prison, and if they persisted, they were tortured and exiled, their belongings confiscated.

It was Decius, then, who launched the idea of a religion of state that sought to marry temporal and spiritual power, and normalized intolerance. He proposed a model of persecution that was taken up and later pursued more brutally, after a period of peace, by the emperors Valerian and Diocletian. While the edict didn't aim exclusively at Christians, it nevertheless incited episodes of hostility against them, so crowds sometimes attacked them as they left their meetings. Most Christians conformed to the edict and sacrificed. As Cyprien, the bishop of Carthage and a Church father, wrote, scandalized, "At the first threatening words of the enemy, the greatest number of our brothers betrayed their faith."[2] Most of those who lapsed, being accustomed to Roman tolerance, did not consider sacrificing to the gods of state as putting into question their membership in the Christian community. Many bishops agreed and saw no difficulty maintaining their faith in Jesus while they sacrificed to the Roman gods, thereby avoiding trouble while preserving their property. Some bishops even turned over relics and sacred texts to the magistrates to maintain their position and escape arrest. Besides, there were different ways you could get a false certificate—for example, by bribing an official or sending someone in your place. The practice of sending a substitute to do the sacrifice (*libellatici*) was not so grave a lapse.

Nevertheless, the condition of so many *lapsi*, those who had obeyed the emperor's order to sacrifice, sowed discord, provoking schisms and eventually heresies in the Church. The question of pardoning or condemning the *lapsi* persisted long after the peace of the Church had ended the persecutions. The question served to nourish and increase the "rigorist current," the orthodox, some would say fanatical branch of the African Church, later led by Donatus, the archbishop of Carthage, for whom only those of the purest, most uncompromising piety would be admitted to the sacraments or be allowed to perform them. At the time of the persecutions of Decius, one of the very first bishops of Arles, Marcianus, was accused of lacking goodness and mercy for refusing to take back the Christians who had betrayed their faith. The "laxists" were eager to be pardoned for their betrayal so they might be rehabilitated as practicing Christians; "rigorists" defended the faith against the least compromise. Several councils held at Carthage debated the extent to which the community should accept these lapsed Christians.

After Decius, Emperor Gallien inaugurated a period of what has been called "the little peace of the Church" in anticipation of "The Peace of the Church," instituted seventy years later by Emperor Constantine. The edict of Gallien was followed shortly by a new period of severe oppression known as the "Great Persecution," conducted under the joint emperors Diocletian and Galerius, who commanded that everyone make sacrifices to the Roman gods or face immediate execution at a burning stake—a novel idea.

In 250 years, between the Great Fires in Rome, which Nero blamed on the Christians, and the Edict of Milan in 313, when Constantine declared Christianity a legitimate religion, there were only four emperors who extensively persecuted Christians. Besides Nero, there were Decius, Diocletian, and Galerius. Local governors had their own hatreds. Diocletian, a brilliant administrator, probably saved the empire from the chaos of the third century. He had ruled peacefully for many years and had authored reforms that changed the structure of Roman imperial government and helped stabilize the empire economically and militarily, enabling it to remain essentially intact for another 150 years despite being near the brink of collapse in his youth.

Near the end of his brilliant, largely tolerant reign, Diocletian was pressured by his junior partner, Galerius, who despised Christians, to launch a general persecution. In 302 the emperors argued over imperial policy toward Christians. Diocletian thought it was enough to appease the gods if Christians were forbidden from the bureaucracy and the military. Galerius argued for their extermination.

Seeking the sun, Diocletian and Galerius holed up together for the winter in the palace at Nicomedia, where Galerius endlessly harangued the emperor, encouraging him to burn Christians. Diocletian was wary, but in the end decided to settle the question by sending one of his haruspex or soothsayers from his palace in Syria to Delphi to seek the opinion of the Pythian oracle of Apollo. In a letter written later to his eastern subjects, Constantine, who at the time was there at court, flatly asserts that emperors who persecuted Christians all came to a bad end. Diocletian and his junior partner stirred the persecutions at a time when the empire was largely at peace. The oracle spoke to the soothsayer from "a certain chamber and dark alcove," but "not out of a human being," that is, not out of the mouth of a priestess. The oracle said it was performing false oracles from the tripods of Apollo because, writes Constantine, "the righteous on earth were an impediment to telling the truth."

This seemed to indicate that the priests of Apollo were lamenting these righteous people as "this evil within human society." Constantine hears Diocletian closely questioning his bodyguards, wanting to know who these righteous people were. One of his soothsayers, probably the haruspex, said that of course they were Christians. On that very spot, the emperor drew up the "edicts of blood and venom."

Diocletian issued an edict ordering Christian churches to be razed and holy articles to be confiscated, and he threatened to deprive Christian senators and nobles of their rank; they risked imprisonment if they did not convert. At the urging of Galerius, he issued a second edict, which ordered the arrest and imprisonment of bishops and priests. The emperor sought a suitable and auspicious day for announcing the edict, and so he chose to issue it on February 23, the last day of the Roman calendar, at the ancient festival of Terminalia, celebrated in honor of the god Terminus, who presided at the boundaries of property. He was often represented not by a statue but by a simple large stone to signal a limit. The end of the year would henceforth mark the end of the Christian religion. The edict prohibited Christians from assembling for worship, and it ordered the destruction of their scriptures, liturgical books, and places of worship across the empire. Christians could not respond to actions brought against them in court; Christian senators, equestrians, decurions, veterans, and soldiers were deprived of their ranks; and Christian freemen were reenslaved.

Christian writers have enormously exaggerated the number of Christian martyrdoms ordered by Roman emperors: altogether, there were only a few thousand. Some actively sought it, for martyrdom was recognized as the exemplary Christian practice, the highest title to which one could aspire; it took the imitation of Christ to the point of wishing to mirror His death. Martyrs became rivals of priests regarding their power of intercession to absolve sinners, and their numbers kept on expanding. The power of the martyrs' blood showed that something fundamental was at stake in the shift from a pagan to a Christian culture—from one in which honor was a higher value even than life to one where dying for your faith was the highest honor. The greatest tragedy of Western civilization was this shift in values from Roman law, with its basis in honor, to Christian martyrdom, with its irrational faith in salvation. For fifteen hundred years and more, your rulers have been in league with priests telling lies and making things up.

Before Christianity became the religion of the state, enforced by imperial decree, and after persecutions ceased, martyrdom was the most specific and powerful advertisement for the faith. Christian blood, it was said, was the seed that inseminated the Church and sparked its growth. At the end of the third century, martyrdom gave Christians their first visibility, before they had yet built any churches. Except for the single instance of persecution after the great fires in Rome in 46, the Church enjoyed two hundred years of relative peace. But it was during that time, which roughly coincided with the life of Favorinus, that the power of a martyr's blood was first revealed by the illustrious self-immolation of Peregrinus, who called himself Proteus, at the 157th Olympiade.

Born a beautiful boy in Armenia, Peregrinus was soon caught in the act of adultery and escaped with only a beating by jumping off a roof. He was next accused of corrupting another handsome boy. He avoided the court of the governor by buying off the boy's poor family. Eager to have his inheritance, but with his father still living, he put a rope around his father's neck and hanged him. When that started to be talked about, he decided to exile himself, and he began wandering from place to place.

In his travels he turned up in Palestine, where he shortly fell in with Christian priests and scribes and soon picked up their "queer creed," as Lucian called it. Christians superstitiously worshipped a man, it was thought, a crucified criminal no less. Peregrinus shortly convinced them that he was their superior in theological knowledge, and they elected him prophet, elder, ruler of the synagogue. He expounded on their books, explained their teachings, and wrote books himself. They took him for a god and accepted his laws. His preaching soon aroused the authorities, which had him arrested and thrown into prison. That made his fortune. The whole Christian community set about trying to free him, in the meantime making his stay in jail as pleasant as possible, transforming it into what the Romans called a *felix carcar*: a happy prison.

In the first centuries of Christianity, it wasn't uncommon for crooks pretending to be Jews to present themselves to rich Christians, declaring their willingness to convert and asking for their support. They were given money, and they were baptized. The new Christians would once again pretend to be Jews and find other victims for their fraud.

Were I to digress, I'd recall the most illustrious instance of felix carcar, which occurred when my sister Mount Pelée, the tallest mountain on Martinique, exploded one day in May 1902. Thirty thousand people, the entire population of Saint-Pierre, the capital city at its foot, were killed in an instant by the fiery cloud of poisonous gas that shot out the side of the mountain and promptly descended on the city. The only survivor was Ludger Sylbaris, a worker who had been thrown into jail overnight after a bar fight. He was the sole inhabitant of the local prison, whose thick walls saved him from the volcano's wrath. Later he joined the Barnum and Bailey circus and become something of a celebrity, thanks to his deliverance. These days, more people than are willing to admit it found the confinement of the pandemic to be a happy prison.

The happiness of Proteus in prison was ensured by the Christians who did everything they possibly could for him. Jailers were bribed, elegant dinners were brought in, sacred writings were read; they considered Peregrinus, as he was still called in those days, to be "the modern Socrates." His fame spread, and Christian communities from far and wide sent expressions of sympathetic support and offers of legal aid. Money came pouring in.

The governor, whose hobby was philosophy, realized that Peregrinus sought publicity for himself above all, even if he had to die for it, so the astute governor set him free. He went back to Armenia, where news of his parricide had circulated, and, feeling unwelcomed, he was shortly obliged to leave. Still under the protection of the Christians, he lacked for nothing and wandered around luxuriously until something he did, a piece of magic or unthinking sacrifice, had him expelled from their cult. Having decided to become a Cynic philosopher, he continued his peregrinations with less and less success, until he arrived in Athens during the Olympics with a vast idea: he published his intention to cremate himself at the next one.

When the time came, he had an enormous pyre built next to the Olympic stadium, and after making a magnificent speech to a large crowd, as night fell, he jumped into the middle of the pyre and was consumed. Peregrinus taught a valuable lesson to later Christian martyrs: there is no martyrdom without good publicity. To suffer martyrdom in a place where no one could observe it did nothing to advance the interests of the faith. And besides, people love nothing more than the theater of self-immolation. The imposing spectacle of his fiery death, in this holy place of the Olympiad, where the gods are appeased, ensured the fame of Proteus throughout the empire. His martyrdom demonstrated the power of blood to attract followers. Sure enough, there were those who claimed that Proteus had cured them of their fevers and that they had encountered in him "the guardian spirit of the night." Soon they were setting up an altar at the scene of the cremation, with nocturnal rites and torchlight processions around the pyre.

Among the many religious cults that flourished in the empire, Christian sects were certainly distinguished by their aggressive proselytizing, for as Pope Paul VI said, not long ago, "Evangelizing is in fact the grace and vocation proper to the Church, her deepest identity. She exists in order to evangelize."[3] Christians responded to the widespread thirst in antiquity for conversion, for a new life, a *vita nuova* that offered the promise of an eternal one, however unthinkable. Even if it were possible, it would be undesirable: in an eternal afterlife there could be no possibility of loss; in an afterlife without loss, nothing would matter.

It was their encouragement of martyrdom that distinguished the early Christian Church from other cults. To seek martyrdom, as some Christians did, was to give incontrovertible evidence of the superior power of their faith in Heaven over faith in this life. For Christians, death was not death, but the gateway to eternal life. The new language of Christianity turned death into sleep and cemeteries into dormitories. The "red crown" of Christian martyrdom promised Heaven, for eternity. The blood they spilled was in such perfect imitation of Christ's that it made them holier even than priests for granting the absolution of sins. Christians superstitiously worshipped relics of their Lord and of his saints. They had a cult of the dead and regularly met in cemeteries. Above all, they had an intense belief in salvation that many philosophers found disgusting.

The persecutions stopped once and for all when Emperor Constantine, in 313, was graced with a vision of what may have been a cross—before his fateful battle at Milvan Bridge outside Rome against his rival, Maxentius. Beneath the Christogram in the sky, Chi Rho (☧, the first two Greek letters in Christos, the sign that later came to be called the *Chrismon*), there was written in Greek *ev τούτῳ níκα* ("in this sign, conquer"). That night, the emperor had a dream in which Christ told him to inscribe the Christogram on the *labarum*, the military standard carried by his soldiers. You know the story. Vastly outnumbered, his auspiciously blessed troops conquered divinely. Constantine was the first to turn the Christian symbol of love and sacrifice into a bloody battle standard.

Out of gratitude for the vision, he issued what became known as the Edict of Milan, which at last guaranteed legitimacy to the Christian community that had only recently been the focus of the Great Persecution by Emperor Diocletian. The edict at last gave them the right to practice their religion alongside the myriad other legitimate cults in the empire on behalf of whom Constantine had decreed freedom of worship. Constantine's edict was an act of generosity that followed a long tradition of polytheistic tolerance of many gods. Despite the claims of Christian propaganda, Christianity did not become the state religion at that moment, and Constantine himself did not then become a Christian, not until much later, on his deathbed. In fact, even at the end of his life, even as he showed preference to Christianity, he encouraged citizens to maintain their traditional beliefs and practices. He never fully understood how inherently exclusive Christianity was, although Jews for centuries had been claiming to be the chosen ones. He could not have foreseen that legitimizing it as one cult among many was the condition of its shortly being established as the single, exclusive, intolerant state religion.

Constantine's generosity toward the formerly persecuted Christians may have resulted, as Christians believe, from his having been given the sign of the cross at the battle of Milvan Bridge. Others believe he was struck by a beam of light sent from the solar deity, Sol Invictus, the unconquerable sun. A third view is that of the pagan historian Zosimus, writing in the sixth century, basing his account on older sources. Once Constantine had cemented his power with victories over his imperial rivals, he no longer concealed his evil disposition and vicious inclinations, says Zosimus. He put to death his oldest son, Crispus, who was rumored to have debauched his mother-in-law, Fausta, the young wife of Constantine. When Helena, the grandmother of Crispus, expressed her sorrow and lamented her grandson's cruel death with much bitterness, Constantine, under the pretense of comforting her, applied a remedy worse than the disease. He caused his wife, Fausta, to be shut up in a bathing room and ordered it heated to an extraordinary degree. He shortly removed her from it, dead.

After a while, Constantine began to feel pangs of conscience, and went to the temples to ask priests to relieve his guilt. But they told him there were no purifications capable of washing away such heinous crimes. Shortly thereafter he encountered a Spaniard named Aegyptius ("very friendly with the court ladies," says Zosimus), who had just arrived at court. Falling into conversation with the emperor, Aegyptius assured him that the Christian doctrine would teach him how to cleanse himself of all his offenses, for they who received it were immediately absolved of all their sins. Jesus loves the repentant sinner. Constantine easily believed what he was told. Forsaking the religious rites of Rome, he accepted those that were now offered him by Christians. The first sign of his impiety, as Zosimus saw it, was his interdiction of fortune-telling and haruspication.

Constantine's legislation of the years 318–321 dealt largely with magic and divination, out of fear, as Zosimus puts it, that others might themselves gain power via those means, as he himself had done, by frequently consulting oracles that correctly predicted his great successes. Although public pagan practices were still explicitly allowed, he now wanted all haruspication—all practices of magic and divination that foretell the future—abolished, says Zosimus.[4] He was afraid that the oracles might foretell something that would then occur to his misfortune—some correct oracle directed against himself, against his own future rule.

Constantine, who was not the sharpest sword in the arsenal, was theologically curious. Raised in the pluralist, tolerant society of his father, Constantius Chlorus (the "Pure" one), he was interested in religion and at times embraced different cults that he richly supported as emperor with gratifying honors and privileges. Not until the end did he resolve the ambivalence of his religious identity. Growing up, he had shared the Platonizing belief of his father in a single supreme being that contained a plurality of other deities, and whom he identified with Sol, the embodiment of the sun. But he was often confused by theological arguments and for a long time hesitated between worshiping Jesus and/or Sol Invictus.

The emperor Aurelian strengthened the position of the sun god as the main divinity of the Roman pantheon. His intention was to give all the peoples of the empire—civilian or soldier, Easterner or Westerner—a single god they could believe in without betraying their own gods. The traditional image of the sun has also been used in early Jewish art. A mosaic floor in Hamat Tiberias presents David as Helios surrounded by a ring with the signs of the zodiac. Some say December 25 was chosen for Christmas because it was the date of the festival of Sol Invictus, with whom Mithras was also identified.

The center of the cult was a new temple that Aurelian built in 274 and dedicated on December 25 of that year in the Campus Agrippae in Rome, with great decorations financed by the spoils of the Palmyrene Empire. Aurelian would be followed by others in his solar piety, in his tolerant politics, and in the intimate conviction that he was the representative of God on Earth.

The Great Persecution of Christians was the most extensive and bloody since Nero, but it failed to eliminate Christianity. Galerius rescinded the edict in 311, announcing that the persecution had failed to bring Christians back to traditional religion. After the Great Persecution there followed an era of tolerance. The cruel edicts were not actually reversed, and peace was not official, until the peace of Emperor Maxentius, in 311, halted the persecution of Christians because of their growing importance in Rome, in Italy, and in the Roman provinces of Africa.

This was the occasion on which were first felt stirrings, since Decius, of what was to become a schism in the church. Christian priests, during the persecutions, were under orders to deliver over to the authorities their Bibles and relics. The faithful were commanded to commit sacrifices to the Roman gods under threat of arrest and execution. As I've said, most Christians, priests and laity, had no trouble, in those polytheistic times, maintaining their membership in the Christian community while performing a little sacrifice for the sake of peace. Just as earlier, some avoided trouble by corrupting magistrates, a few fled or went into hiding, and others paid to send a replacement. Later, however, after persecutions had definitively ended, the strictly orthodox Christians again refused to accept back into their community those who had lapsed. The orthodox were led by the Berber Christian bishop of Carthage, Donatus Magnus, who affirmed that the validity of the sacraments depended on the moral character of the minister. Lapsed priests, by definition, were not among the moral. The so-called pure Christians called the lapsed priests *traditores*, which signified "deliverer of sacred objects" as well as "traitor." They were certainly influenced by the writings of their North African Christian compatriots, Tertullian and Cyprian of Carthage, who argued that Christians who had compromised the faith with pagan sacrifices and were then reintegrated into the community ought to be forbidden from becoming priests. And similarly, priests who had delivered up their holy writings or themselves performed sacrifices lost all spiritual authority, and their sacraments were without value.

The troubles that arose between the Donatists and the lapsed members of the Church soon began to alarm the emperor in Rome. Bands of fanatical monks from their desert retreats swooped down into Alexandria and attacked pagans and the enemies of the rigorist archbishop. Hypatia was their most esteemed and celebrated victim. To this day I am outraged at the witless misogyny and vile ignorance of monks and priests who deprived the ancient world of its greatest woman mathematician in the name of their superstition. Hypatia's death marked the end of paganism and the triumph of Christianity after hundreds of years of war against Greco-Roman culture.

Constantine thought he could resolve what he took to be a minor theological problem with appeals to the pope in Rome, who in response summoned eighteen bishops from Italy and Gaul to come to the Vatican to condemn the Donatists, who were later deemed to be schismatic on the way to heresy, the first such heresy to be formally condemned by the Church.

Constantine comes to establish the peace of the Church but especially peace in the Church. At Nicea, he says: "I also am a bishop; while you are the bishops of those within the church, I am the bishop of the outside"—a claim to be the spiritual leader of Christianity. He assumes the role of a Roman *pon-*

tifex maximus but a Christian one, authorized not only to rewrite dogma but even to grant clerical titles and alter rituals. The pope was not invited and had no representative there in Arles; Constantine had also now become the unofficial head of the Church. Like St. Paul, he had had a vision of the Cross and was determined to spread the word, to "exterminate vice and theological error."

The Donatists appealed to Constantine the Great against the decision of the Council of Rome in 313 at the Lateran under Pope Miltiades. The appeal was rejected, and the Donatists henceforth became the enemy of Rome. Open conflict broke out in Carthage over the successor to the "laxist" Bishop Mensurias. The Donatists protested the nomination of Caecilianus, who had been ordained by Mensurias, whom they considered a *traditore*. According to the "rigoristes," his ordination was invalid, so he could not become a bishop. Led by Donatus, seventy North African bishops elected a rival bishop, Majorinus. As Donatus obstinately persisted in contesting the ordination of a priest by a lapsed bishop, Constantine determined to look for a more consequential, imperial solution. The emperor found his man in Arles.

The archbishop of Arles, the most powerful cleric in Gaul, a certain Marinus, had devoted his life's work to stamping out pagan practices and reinforcing the power of the emperor, who had a palace in Arles. Marinus had begun by trying to shut down the arena and put an end to gladiator games. There was enormous resistance in Arles among the people who loved them. For centuries the games had been used as instruments of imperial power by emperors, who gained people's favor with gifts of bloody spectacles. In collaboration with Constantine, who was more interested in keeping the peace in North Africa than in theological argument, Marinus devised the idea of a council in which all the senior bishops and archbishops would democratically vote—one man, one vote—on issues of Christian doctrine. The notion prevailed in all these and subsequent councils that a majority vote of the electors expressed the will of God. In principle, everyone had an equal vote. In practice, the highest-ranking bishops had their clans. Despite the appearance of democracy, it was the will of the most powerful that prevailed—under the eye of Constantine.

The first of August 314, a year after Constantine had legitimized Christianity, he was persuaded by Marinus to convoke a council of bishops (a hundred representatives of forty-four churches) in order to anathematize Donatism. There were nine from North Africa, ten from Italy, six from Spain, three from Britain and Brittany, and sixteen from Gaul. The provincial churches sent three bishops (from Arles, Marseille, and Vaison), and three dioceses (Apt, Nice, and Orange) sent only clerics. The emperor leaped at the opportunity to use the orthodox church, just emerged from persecutions, to condemn the Christian rebels in North Africa. Marinus used the occasion shrewdly to increase the influence over the emperor of this recently despised and persecuted religion. More importantly, it was the first moment in the fatal linking of the hierarchical Christian church to imperial Roman politics. Whenever intolerant Christianity is joined to political power, it becomes tyrannical. It is still a menace.

Arles thus became the site of the first ever ecumenical council, the forerunner of the First Council of Nicea, which codified the orthodox doctrine of the Trinity. The council took place on top of me over there in the church of Notre-Dame-de-la-Major, which had been thrown up over the ruins of the adorable temple of Bona Dea. Besides condemning the heresy of Donatism, the council excommunicated its author. It took other consequential decisions as well. It decreed canonically:

Easter should be celebrated on the same day around the world, rather than being left to the decision of local bishops.

It forbade people from participating in chariot races or gladiatorial games, on pain of excommunication. (Marinus achieved his dream; the people of Arles were devastated.)

It forbade the rebaptism of heretics who repudiated their heresy.

The ordination of priests required the participation of three bishops.

Finally, and most crucially, it declared that clergy who, during the persecutions, had handed over to the authorities sacred books and relics (the so-called *traditores*) were to be defrocked, but their official acts (in particular, performing the sacraments) were considered legitimate.

The Council of Arles ended on the first of August 314, and its decisions acquired the force of law when the emperor promulgated them three years later. He also ordered the dissolution of the Donatist community and the confiscation of their wealth.

The Council of Arles was the first ecumenical council but not the last. The very next one, the Council of Nicea, was the most important of all. It fixed the orthodox doctrine of the Church concerning the Trinity. It decreed against the view of those like Bishop Arius, who argued that because Jesus was born into the world, a created being, he was therefore secondary, subordinate, consequently less than what came before him, namely the Father; Jesus, the son, is hence more than human, less than fully divine. Against that reasonable doctrine, the Council of Nicea promulgated the doctrine of co-substantiality. Jesus is the son of God but doesn't come from God; in no way is Jesus junior, secondary, subordinate. All three, the Father, the Son, and the Holy Ghost, share the same substance, have the same being: in Greek, *homoousia*.

It's always been a puzzle to me how Arianism lost the battle with the Nicene Creed. It must be for the very reason that the idea of the co-substantial Trinity confounds all logic and sense, thereby requiring an absolute, unshakable act of faith. Or maybe the Arian Trinity had an odor of polytheism.

There were by that time, particularly in North Africa, a great many Donatist communities that resisted the application of Constantine's laws. They provoked violence in Carthage and other African provinces. After a few years, unable to impose calm on the situation, Constantine lifted the repressive measures while the Donatists remained even more faithful to their *"rigoriste"* theology, having recently suffered so much on its behalf. They thought of themselves as the only ones who remained pure, like the children of martyrs without compromise, in the face of the sons of *traditores*.

From that point on, successive Christian emperors more and more severely persecuted pagan practices and destroyed pagan temples. There were fewer than fifty years from the time of Constantine the Great until the end of the fourth century, when Emperor Theodosius interdicted by punishment of death the practice of pagan sacrifices and outlawed all pagan cults. He took further measures to suppress paganism in the Roman Empire. He issued his edict in 391, the same year that the Serapeum, the great temple of Zeus in Alexandria, was destroyed.

Finally, the Olympic Games were canceled after the last ones were held in 393;[5] they were regarded by the emperor as a pagan practice, which they were (are they still?). Olympic games, like gladiator games, had their distant origin in honoring the deceased. The first recorded Olympic game, a single footrace, was in 776 BCE, but Greek games had been going on since Homer. They continued every four years for more than a thousand years. They were the occasion in antiquity on which the Greek world celebrated Zeus, the king of the gods, whose court resided on the sacred Mount Olympus. In the middle of the games, they paused to honor the god with a hecatomb, the sacrifice of a hundred oxen. The sacred character of the games was reflected in the *ekecheiria*, the Olympic truce called across Greece that forbade the city-states, even if at war, from hindering athletes or spectators or judges from going and coming to the games.

Banning the Olympics at the end of the fourth century could be taken to mark the triumph of Christianity, the end of paganism as an official practice. Among the people there remained bits of personal paganism; amulets, oaths, and superstitions survived, as we have seen, for centuries in the hearts of people in Arles. One still glimpses pagan passions at the bullfights and in the riot of the feria. But the Christian emperor left nothing undone when it came to dismantling the official practices of the Roman Empire.

After the fall of the empire, the Church didn't neglect to undo centuries of tolerance of Jews—except for a while in Arles, where the archbishop was their protector and benefactor. They enriched the city with their talents— until the fifteenth century.

Here the Rock paused the story before going on in the next session to tell the bittersweet story of the Jews in Arles.

VIII

A Worthy Woman

[אשה הנוגה]

It's true, of course, that the earliest sign of the presence of Jews near Arles is the little oil lamp decorated with a menorah found at Orgon, a village near Cavaillon in the Alpilles. Somebody left it there in the first century. You might wonder what Jews were doing up there in the hills. In those days they were often workers in the field. Jews had been here even earlier, following Greeks and Romans around the Mediterranean for centuries. Legend has it that after the destruction of the Second Temple in 70, Emperor Vespasian loaded three boats full of Jewish captives and sent them off rudderless across the Mediterranean without a captain or crew. Propelled by random winds, one boat landed at Bordeaux, another at Lyon, the third at Arles. The legend accounts for the origin of three main centers of Jewish life in Gaul; it doesn't explain how they sailed over land so far north and west. Jews had been tolerated—even welcomed—in Arles for centuries before Christianity became the state religion. The Romans didn't even have a word for tolerance; it was taken for granted. For centuries, they treated Jews the way they treated all the other legitimate cults, even allowing them their peculiar claim to exclusivity, to being the chosen people of God.

Once Emperor Constantine saw the Christogram in the sky, and under it conquered, he began showering favors on the recently persecuted Christians, even as he abandoned the generous tolerance of his father's reign. In a letter to bishops who were unable to attend the Council of Nicea, he warned them against permitting the Easter holiday to conflict with the Jewish Passover. He admonished them against participating in the seder, as many early Jewish Christians were inclined to do:

> "It was improper," wrote the emperor, "to follow the custom of the Jews in celebration of their holy festivals because, their hands having been stained by crime [*killing Jesus*], the minds of these wretched men are necessarily blinded.... Let us therefore have nothing in common with the Jews, who are our enemies, let us studiously avoid all contact with their evil way ... a senseless people so utterly depraved."[1]

He considered "senseless" the people who wrote the Bible; "depraved" were the Jews, who observed 613 laws.

As Christian emperors consolidated their religious authority, they needed more and more to separate themselves from Jews who were great preachers and attracted converts. The narcissism of minor differences (which leads you to hate the most those you most closely resemble) ensured that Christians feared and despised the Jews above all the many cults in Rome. St. John Chrysostom, he of the golden mouth, an early Church father, declared concerning Jews: "Although such beasts are unfit for work, they are fit for killing. And this is what happened to the Jews: while they were making themselves unfit for work, they grew fit for slaughter." In this, he follows Jesus when he said: "But as for these my enemies, who did not want me to be king over them, bring them here and slay them."[2] On the strength of his reading of the Psalms, St. John states that the Jews "sacrificed their sons and daughters to devils: they outraged nature; and overthrew from their foundations the laws of relationship. They are become worse than the wild beasts, and for no reason at all, with their own hands, they murder their own offspring, to worship the devil."[3]

Despite the hatred of Constantine and the Church fathers who considered them "enemies," Jews had it pretty good in Arles. The great archbishop of Arles, St. Hilaire, died shortly after Emperor Valentinian III had decreed the first anti-Jewish Roman laws, prohibiting local Jews from entering the magistracy, from possessing Christian slaves, or from taking careers of arms. (Jews used to be considered good fighters.) Christ himself attended the funeral of St. Hilary and left an imprint of his heel on a stone coffin. Or was that the funeral of St. Trophime? I can't say. I didn't see a thing. The grief at the burial was so unspeakable among the Christians of Arles that in their silence at the Alyscamps cemetery the only sound was the weeping and wailing of the Jews. People remarked how strange it was to hear the psalms sung in Hebrew.

St. Trophime was the first bishop of Arles. He had been sent by St. Paul [*in 42*] to convert the barbarians. He used to gather a little group of Christians in the Alyscamps, the way the first Christians in Rome met in the catacombs among the skeletons. He hid from the pagans until he revealed himself as a Christian when he stepped into the arena to stop the public sacrifice of two infants. He built the first oratory or house of prayer, which he dedicated to the protomartyr, the first Christian martyr, St. Etienne, whose relics Trophime had brought with him from Jerusalem.

From there, things went from bad to worse for the Jews as the Church assumed hegemony. Emperor Theodosius and his son Theodosius II deprived the Jews of the few rights they had reserved and imposed new taxes and obligations. In an edict addressed to Amatius, prefect of Gaul [*in 425*], they prohibited Jews and pagans from practicing law, from holding public offices or being soldiers (*militandi*), "in order that Christians should not be subjected to them, and thus be incited to change their faith." The Council of Vannes [*in 465*] forbade the clergy to share the meals of the Jews or to invite them to their own, because the Christian clergy would appear inferior to them if they accepted Jewish food, while the Jews refused to eat the food that Christians offered them. This prohibition was repeated at the Council of Agda [*in 506*], again at the Council of Epaon, and once more at the third Council of Orleans. It was either the excellence of Jewish cooking in the sixth century or the well-known gluttony of clerics that elicited so many repeated exhortations.

The second Council of Orleans [*533*], that of Clermont [*535*], and that of Orleans [*538*] prohibited all intermarriage of Jews and Christians. Christians who would not agree to dissolve such unions were to be excommunicated.

The third Council of Orleans [*538*] and again that of Mâcon [*581*] decreed that "since, by the grace of God, we live under the rule of Catholic kings, the Jews should not appear among Christians for four consecutive days after Good Friday."

The fourth Council of Orleans [*541*] decreed, among other things, that whenever a Jew set out to convert a Christian or reconvert to his religion a Jew who had been baptized, or had acquired a Christian slave, or converted to Judaism anyone born of Christian parents, he should be punished by the loss of all his slaves.

If anyone born of Christian parents became a Jew, and obtained his freedom on condition of remaining such, the condition must be considered void, for it was unjust that one living as a Jew should enjoy the freedom attaching to Christians.

To the prohibition against appearing in public during Holy Week were added the obligation to show reverence to ecclesiastes and the interdiction against walking before them. Those who broke this law were to be punished by the local magistrate.

The Council of Narbonne forbade Jews to sing psalms at burials of their own people; those who transgressed this decree were compelled to pay a fine to the lord of the city.

The fifth Council of Paris [614] prohibited Jews from seeking or from exercising civic or administrative rights over Christians unless they and their families should accept baptism from the bishop of the place. The same prohibition was renewed at the Council of Reims in 624–625. This council returned to the question of Christian slaves and decreed that if a Jew converted or tormented his Christian slaves, they should revert to the state treasury.

After 476, the date when the last Roman emperor was deposed, Arles was ruled by its archbishop, St. Césaire, who brilliantly held off the barbarians as well as Alaric, the king of the Goths, who now governed Gaul. He was constantly exhorting his flock: "Each Sunday, you must go to church. If the miserable Jews celebrate their sabbath with such great devotion that they do no material thing on that day, how much stronger is the reason that Christians have on the Lord's Day to consecrate themselves to God alone and gather in church for the salvation of their soul."[4]

When the archbishop was accused of conspiring with the king of Burgundy to betray the city, he cleverly deflected the charge by having a henchman forge a letter that convicted the Jews of treachery. The henchman threw the compromising letter over the walls, where it was found by guards. It conveniently included the name and the sect of the traitor. The Jew was executed; St. Césaire was absolved and reinstated. He took the opportunity to chase the Jews out of Arles, not for the last time. It's not the only reason the fascists of Vichy adored him.

Archbishop Virgilus, bishop of Arles, displayed such zeal for the salvation of Jewish souls that Pope Gregory the Great thought it necessary to censure him for having baptized Jews by force. He must desist, he wrote:

Many of the Jews settled in those parts have been brought to the font of baptism more by force than by preaching. Now, I consider the intention in such cases to be worthy of praise ... but I fear lest this same intention, unless adequate enforcement from Holy Scripture accompany it, should either have no profitable result. ... For, when any one is brought to the font of baptism, not by the sweetness of preaching, but by compulsion, he returns to his former superstition, and dies the worse from having been born again. Let, therefore, your Fraternity stir up such men by frequent preaching.[5]

Despite the pope's admonition, a great many Jews were converted by force over the course of the next few centuries. Things didn't really improve for them until the eighth century, when Charlemagne and his descendants came to power in Gaul. Under the tolerant reign of the Carolingian dynasty, the Jewish community in Arles found at last some stability, some security within their neighborhood down by the river. Eventually, much later, when they were regularly being attacked during famines by desperate peasants, they built a wall around the *rue de la Juiverie* behind which they had their often-large multi-family houses and synagogue.

By the twelfth and thirteenth centuries, the Jewish community was thriving economically. They were spared persecution by Christian crusaders because they were protected by the archbishop under whom by law they served. Jews were the principal brokers up and down the Rhône facilitating trade in the region, with its vast agricultural production and customers around Gaul and beyond. All the Jews of Arles were moneylenders, big and small. The Church anathematized making money with money.

Some Jews exercised professions that required a certain higher education. They were the only bookbinders in town; they also kept the books of many merchants and collected fees for them. Most of the doctors in Arles were Jews, as were most of the midwives. Jewish doctors could often read Greek, Latin, Hebrew, and Arabic, giving them access to a wealth of medical literature from Ancient Greek and Arab sources that were unavailable to their Christian colleagues. The authorities had trouble even finding Christian doctors. Even though Jews were officially prevented from treating Christians, the ban was generally ignored. Christians needed them; the archbishop kept one on the payroll.

In the twelfth and thirteen centuries, Arles became a great center of Jewish intellectual life that produced a famous family of learned men, the Tibbonides. Judah ben Saul was the father whose son Samuel had a son, Moses, who had a son, Judah, whose son, like his fathers before him, practiced translation from the Arabic into Hebrew of Greek scientific and philosophical works that had been lost after the fall of Rome. The family were commentators and defenders of Maimonides, the controversial twelfth-century Jewish philosopher who brought Aristotle and logic to Hebrew theology. The followers of Maimonides not only proved that Aristotle was compatible with the Torah but also that Aristotle, if not himself a Jew, as some maintained, had nevertheless learned everything he knew from the Jews—aside from a few details. Simon the Just is cited as the man who claimed the honor of having converted Aristotle to Judaism.

In the Arabic *Letter of the Animals* [also known as *The Animals' Lawsuit against Humanity*], translated into Hebrew by Ḳalonymus ben Ḳalonymus, all the members of the animal kingdom—from horses to bees—come before the Spirit King to eloquently complain of the cruel treatment they had suffered at the hands of humans. When a Greek human boasts that his nation is the very embodiment of science and philosophy, the animals reply: "From whence would you have gotten your philosophy and knowledge, of which you boast so much, if not from the Israelites in the time of Ptolemy, and from the Egyptians in the time of Themistus? You then carried them to your own land and claimed them as original."[6] Another, more recent version of that story suggests that it was Phoenician sailors who brought their Black Athena from Africa to Mycenean Greece and sparked the African Jewish origins of Greek thought.

The founder of the Tibbonides clan, Judah ben Saul ibn Tibon, established the Jewish school of Lunel near Montpellier, where medicine was taught, among other disciplines. It eventually became the Ecole de Médecine in Montpellier, the oldest and best-known medical school in France.

Benjamin de Tudèle, the traveling rabbi of the twelfth century, visited many of the Jewish communities in the Midi to describe the customs and practices of their synagogues, and to record their many Talmudic schools, their great teachers, and their masters. Visiting Arles at the end of the twelfth century, he evaluated the Jewish population of Arles at two hundred families, then figured six per family. He names several of the Jews, one of whom, Solomon ben Samuel, was called the *Archi-episcopalis* because he was an official jurist for the archbishop and belonged to his "family." Solomon didn't live in Jew Street [*rue de la Juiverie*] down by the river, but in the center of town facing the cathedral of Saint-Trophime in what was later a splendid noble house of the Astruc family, one of the city's great Jewish fortunes.

Although Jews were excluded from Arlesian citizenship, they were not considered foreigners. They had their own cemetery north of the Alyscamps but were not obliged to live in a reserved quarter. The statutes of the city didn't prescribe any social discrimination, like wearing an insignia—the yellow wheel. Jews at that moment were able to engage in agriculture as much as trade, but they were specialists in the commerce of luxury goods: spices, silks, furs. They received from the nearby Abbey of Montmajour the monopoly on the sale of vermillion. Vermillion in the Middle Ages came from the dried eggs of an insect, *Kermes vermilio*, found on oak trees in the Camargue that yielded the deep purple dye that bishops required for their ecclesiastical garments.

Of all the Jews of Arles, the one I love the most—you might have guessed— is the aforementioned Ḳalonymus ben Ḳalonymus, one of the most brilliant and brilliantly perverse of all the Jews in the Sephardic literary tradition. He began his career when he was only twenty years old and soon became a highly regarded writer of original texts and the most productive of the fourteenth-century translators in Arles. He was also a chronicler of the expulsions of Jews from France and of the book burnings of the Talmud in the early fourteenth century. The Christian Church was constantly condemning the Talmud for obscenity and blasphemy (i.e., for allegedly evoking Jesus in Hell "boiling in shit" [tzoah ragochat/צוֹאָה רוֹתַחַת]), which led to multiple book burnings. The first and most famous book burning was in Paris in 1242, when twenty-four cartloads were immolated.

Ḳalonymus ben Ḳalonymus was born here down by the river, in *la Juiverie*. He was the son of Ḳalonymus ben Weir, a prominent "prince" of the Jewish community, scion of a distinguished family that had branches all over Europe. A scholar and a poet, Ḳalonymus traveled widely and lived in many places: Salon, Aix, Barcelona, Rome, Naples. He settled at the end of his life in Avignon, where he became a member of the court of Robert of Anjou, king of Naples, who happened to hear of his great talent as a translator of scientific books and so sent him, provided with letters of recommendation, on a scientific mission to Rome. The learning and character of Ḳalonymus so impressed the Roman notables that when his family wrote to them regretting his absence and demanding his return, the great Hebrew poet Immanuel the Roman [*an imitator of Dante who introduced the Italian sonnet into Hebrew*] wrote a letter to Nasi Samuel, a "prince" of the Jews in Arles, protesting in the name of the Jewish community of Rome against Ḳalonymus's return. Ḳalonymus was the poet referred to by Immanuel as having pleaded the cause of the Roman Jews before the pope at Avignon in 1321.

Kalonymus died in Spain sometime after 1328.

You may know that in 1306, King Philip of France banished the Jews from his kingdom, to which Arles at the time did not yet belong. Many Jews sought refuge there, where the Jews were protected by the archbishop, to whom they paid fees and taxes. During the banishment, while other Jews were fleeing for their lives, Kalonymus tranquilly pursued his original literary writing and his immense work of translation. His translations from the Arabic included Galen's work on bleeding, as well as his immense treatise on enemas and colic; Archimedes's on the sphere and the cylinder; Ptolemy's treatise on the planets; and one on plants, attributed to Aristotle. He also translated Al-Kindi's treatise on humidity and the influence of the heavenly bodies on rain. He translated many commentaries by Averroes (on Aristotle, on his *Metaphysics*, on sophisms), as well as Al-Farabi's treatise on the method of studying philosophy. His work and that of generations of Arlesian translators represent an important moment in the first and perhaps the more important Renaissance, the one that began in the twelfth century, when Greek science and thought, after centuries of ignorance, began to penetrate the minds of Christian Europe.

Although the Rock of Arles never moves, I am sometimes moved by unexpected acts of courage or eruptions of beautiful language. Kalonymus is the author of an extraordinary poem, titled in Hebrew "Eben Boḥan" [אבן בחן—*literally, "Stone Test," that is, "Touchstone." A touchstone is a piece of fine-grained dark schist or jasper formerly used for testing alloys of gold by observing the color of the mark that they made on it. Figuratively, it is a standard for the criterion by which something is judged or recognized.*] Written toward the end of his life, it is the boldest and certainly the most beautiful expression of queer desire in the entire Provençal Sephardic tradition. As far as I know, it may be the only one. I say queer, because it's not simply about the desire of a man to lie with another man, as Leviticus twice proscribes, even though some homosexual readers want to read it that way.

Leviticus 18 and 20 are unambiguous: "And you shall not lie with another male as with a woman." Of course, there have been those gays who have naughtily taken that to mean that Leviticus only prohibits anal sex—tops and bottoms. For five thousand years, ever since the Bronze Age, orthodox rabbis have refused to make allowances for even the least suggestion of same-sex desire. They never even mention lesbian love. The rabbinic tradition down to this day has barely budged. If you go to your Orthodox rabbi to seek advice about the feelings you've been having toward other men, he will tell you to get married: "It'll pass." Or he'll tell you to go see a therapist who will convert you, pervert your perversion to fulfill the Lord's commandment. It never works for long without a lot of misery. Reform rabbis are different; many of them are gay.

Explicit homosexual love in secular Hebrew poetry has a long tradition; since the tenth and eleventh centuries in Spain, many Jewish poets, like Arab ones, have expressed their love for beautiful boys. What is more, Jews in the thirteenth century recognized what we call intersexes: a *tumtum* [טומטום: "hidden"] refers to a person whose sex is unknown because their genitalia are covered or otherwise unrecognizable. (Does that simply mean, like Favorinus, their testicles are undescended?) An *androgynos* [אנדרוגינוס] has both male and female genitalia.

In this poem, "Eben Boḥan," Ḳalonymus confronts and confounds the profound, intractable male bias of Jewish culture—the sexism that comforts Jewish men every morning when they are expected to pray: "Blessed are thou, Lord, our God, ruler of the universe, who has not created me a woman." The poet's voice in "Eben Boḥan," I'll call him Ḳalonymus, prays for the opposite! He cries out to his mother, not exactly to curse her, but to pity himself for having a mother who bore a son who is himself:

> Woe to me, my mother, that you ever bore a son!
> What a great loss and with no benefit!

The idea that being born male to a Jewish mother could be a pure loss—loss without any gain—seems unthinkable, when for thousands of years the covenant with Israel's God has depended on the circumcision of males. But the poet resists the covenant with Hashem, even as he undergoes the knife:

> Uncircumcised of heart and flesh was I born.
> At three days, they cut my umbilical
> cord, and at eight days my foreskin.
> However, my ears, heart, and mind remained uncircumcised
> and were not ready for Hashem's covenant.

Ḳalonymus cries out with pity for unlucky parents whose male children are condemned to obey the 613 commandments of Moses, all the while studying the Talmud from morning to night:

> Woe to him who has male sons.
> Upon them a heavy yoke has been placed

of restrictions and constraints...
Severe statutes and awesome commandments, six hundred and
    thirteen.
Who is the man who is capable
Of fulfilling them all to the letter?
How will he escape
Be he diligent or lazy?

He could have escaped from this cruel fate only by being born as a fair and
decent woman:

Oh, but had the artisan who made
        me created
Me instead—a worthy woman [הנוגה השא].

Imagining his life as a woman, and the benefits it would bring, he dreams
first of the intellectual pleasure, the subtle and penetrating wisdom he would
acquire from the casual, seemingly frivolous conversation of other women,
what some might call the philosophy of the sewing circle. If I had been born
a woman, he writes:

Today I would be wise and insightful.
        We would weave, my friends,
        And in the moonlight spin our
            yarn from dusk till midnight.
        We'd tell the events of our day,
            silly things, matters of no consequence,
        But also, I would grow very
            wise from the spinning, and I would say,
        "How lucky am I to know
            how to make linen."

Making linen brings her wisdom when it's done in a spinning circle with other
women talking idly. How many men, even today, understand the intellectual power of women talking among themselves? Ḳalonymus understands
the education of women who grow wise not by poring over the Talmud all
day but by telling each other things that men find foolish and pointless. Their
talk has no consequences, no point or aim, unlike the talk of men doing business or scholars making arguments. Women spin and weave their yarns into
fine open, lacy fabrics like the intricate web of their thoughts. How lucky

is she who knows how to weave lace! And do embroidery, designing poetic forms:

> cup-like buds, open flowers, cherubim, palm trees,
> and all sorts of other fine things,
> colorful embroideries and furrow-like stitches . . .

Furrow-like, the stitches themselves are like lines of verse running across a page. You know that the word *verse* comes from the Latin *versus*, past participle of the verb *vetere*, which means to turn your plow at the end of a furrow. What makes a poem a verse is the turn at the end of the line.

Why do I, a heartless rock, find this so moving? It seems so unimaginable that a Jewish man in the thirteenth century could so deeply love what Baudelaire called the *mundus muliebris*, the universe of women, that he could imagine and embrace with such loving admiration the feelings of everyday life led by Jewish women in communities austerely ruled by men.

It's been said by Freud that the only technology invented by women is plaiting and weaving:

> It seems that women have made few contributions to the discoveries and inventions in the history of civilization; there is, however, one technique which they may have invented—that of plaiting and weaving. If that is so, we should be tempted to guess the unconscious motive for the achievement. Nature herself would seem to have given the model which this achievement imitates by causing the growth at maturity of the pubic hair that conceals the genitals. The step that remained to be taken lay in making the threads adhere to one another [braiding], while on the body they stick into the skin and are only matted together. If you reject this idea as fantastic and regard my belief in the influence of the lack of a penis on the configuration of femininity as an idée fixe, I am of course defenseless.[7]

You might think this means that spinning and weaving are taken to be minor technologies. But then you should consider that textiles are texts: they illustrate the general idea of text—an interconnected web of elements in which every thread acquires significance only in relation to the others to which it is joined. Each thread in a textile/text points beyond itself; every warp implies a woof.

Not everything, in my view, is a text. If you come across a rock in the forest, it's not textual, unless you're a geologist who can tell its story (or are yourself a rock like me). If you come upon a rock in the forest for the first time, the rock at first glance is just a rock. But if you're a member of the tribe that lives in the forest and knows the rock, you would understand it to be pointing beyond itself, as containing a hidden web of implications and allusions that mark the path back to the others. If you take it as more than the rock that it nevertheless remains, if you understand it as a marker to be read, pointing beyond itself in one direction, it is not just a rock; it is a text. If women can be said to have invented textiles/texts, then they can be said to have invented technology itself, invented invention.

The poet dreams of being a woman among her friends, spinning their yarns "from dusk to midnight"—by the light of the moon. Jews, in general, especially Jewish women, have a special relation to the moon. That hasn't always been true. Synagogues in Palestine from the fourth to the seventh century regularly displayed mosaics on the floor of their entrance with the sun god Helios at their center figured as Sol Invictus surrounded by the signs of the zodiac. But whereas the Roman Empire tended more and more to universal sun worship, Jews after the triumph of Christianity increasingly identified with the moon, reflecting their humbler, dependent status in society. By the twelfth century, the identification with the moon was complete. As the Talmud says, "The other nations count by the sun, while Israel counts by the moon" [*Sukkah 29a*]. The lunar calendar of the Jews calculates the beginning of each month on the new moon, which means that holidays arrive each year on the same days of the month. For at least two thousand years, Jewish women have celebrated the appearance of the new moon with their own special holiday by refraining from spinning, weaving, or doing needlework. On the first night and day of the month, women were free of family chores, a little vacation they honored religiously. In some places, women would gather to light candles (recalling the signal fires lit by the Sanhedrin in Jerusalem to announce to Israel the first hour of the new month).

Whereas sunlight shines only from the surface of the sun, said the rabbis, it is transformed into something more inward, more beautiful when it is reflected by the moon—a more secret, lambent, liquid light, like that at the heart of precious stones. "The sun holds the light that extends outward, whereas the moon holds the light of being," wrote Rav Isaac of Homil [*Shnei Me'orot*].

> And at times, in the way of women,
> I would lie down on the kitchen floor,
> Between the ovens, turn the coals, and
>   taste the different dishes.

What men consider abjection, lying on the floor, turning the coals, is embraced by Ḳalonymus as the way of women. Making beauty and exercising taste is what women do, from below.

> On holidays I would put on my best jewelry, would beat on the drum
> And my clapping hands would ring.

In this sexed and gendered world, a woman was defined by the jewelry she wore (or didn't). Rebecca received the servant of Isaac, who came bearing jewelry for his master's future wife.

Jewelry was the first form of property possessed by women. Weapons are the first property belonging to men. All sexual differences follow from that original division. What gives a woman power over men is her gift of beauty, inspiring admiration and gratitude in those she delights with the glittering figure she cuts, beautifully adorned. Beautiful jewelry is the image (and ringing sound) of radiating brilliance with which the wearer dazzles the spectator as she dances, clapping her hands, emitting an almost palpable aura that causes the will of those who encounter it to submit to its devastating radiance. Like Baudelaire, he is ravished into ecstasy by this shining world of metal and stone, furiously in love with things in which sound and light intermingle.

Then the fantasy goes wildly sexual. He imagines himself being taken as a newlywed:

> And when I was ready and the time was right,

When would he be ready and when would the time ever be right? How would he know?

> An excellent youth would be my fortune.
> He would love me, place me on a pedestal,

Ḳalonymus aspires to promotion as an idol, an icon, like the lady of courtly love, who in the twelfth and thirteenth centuries was being celebrated all around Gaul. Troubadour poets like Peire Vidal at that very time were singing the beauty of the country "enclosed between the Rhône, the Durance, and the sea"—that is to say, the provincial kingdom of Arles. He is haunted by the beauty of an Arlésienne whose memory "leaves men smiling."

> There's no place so sweet as there
> From the Rhône as far as Vence,
> Between the sea and the Durance,

There's no such sweet joy anywhere.
So that with those good people I find
I've left my joyful heart behind
With her who leaves men smiling.
[*literally: With her who makes angry/grieving men laugh*]

[*Qu'om no sap tan dous repaire*
Cum de Rozer tro c'a Vensa,
Si cum clau mars e Durensa,
Ni on tant fins jois s'esclaire.
Per qu'entre la franca gen
Ai laissat mon cor jauzen
Ab lieis que fals iratz rire.][8]

The fantasy of Ḳalonymus gets wilder and wilder, and the poem becomes a sort of epithalamium, a marriage hymn, as he imagines the day—"the appointed day," a day of joy—when the world gathers to celebrate the wedding of Ḳalonyma (now a bride), drenched in jewels, married to her (!) excellent youth:

Dress me in jewels of gold,
Earrings, bracelets, necklaces.
And on the appointed day,
In the season of joy when brides are wed,
For seven days would the boy increase my Delight and
            Gladness.

"Delight" and "Gladness," he writes, not just pleasureful delights but joyful happiness that comes with heartfelt commitment and deepening love. This is a husband who will generously attend to her needs, treat her with kindness, and satisfy her sexually. He gives her better bread, well kneaded, and to drink, two kinds of wine:

Were I hungry, he would feed me well-kneaded bread.
Were I thirsty, he would quench me with light and dark wine.
He would not chastise nor harshly treat me, and my [sexual]
            pleasure he would not diminish.

Ḳalonymus, becoming a woman, acknowledges the reality of his abjection, the fall into subservience that living as a woman entailed in that world, and often in ours. In this fantasy of a husband, s/he would remain desirable, and he would treat her gently, even sweetly. In his dream of becoming a worthy woman, Ḳalonymus would escape the consequences of female abjection. She embraces her dependent condition in relation to a husband who four or five times a month lays his head on her breast and sweetly assumes the pose of her child:

> Every Sabbath, and each new moon,
> His head would he rest upon my breast.

They fulfill their mutual duties of husband and wife, each willingly accepting conventional responsibilities—his to feed and clothe and be regularly intimate with his "wife." She on her side watches carefully for the first signs of menstrual blood [*!?*] to respect the taboo against having sex profaned by menstruation. Her duty is to light the Sabbath candles and braid the Sabbath loaf of sweet challah bread. Ḳalonymus dreams not merely of changing sex but of becoming a good wife who gladly fulfills her duties toward a husband who fulfills his:

> The three husbandly duties he would fulfill,
> Rations, raiment, and regular intimacy.
> And three wifely duties would I also fulfill,
> Sweeter than honey are these three, so powerful,
> And one is not allowed to add to their number,
>   or to inquire about them:
> "Whereby do women earn merit?"

For Ḳalonymus, the desire to become a woman has a moral dimension, not only a psychosexual one. Freed in imagination from the onerous duties and obligations of Jewish men, he nevertheless embraces the duties and responsibilities of a Jewish woman.

There follows a passionate appeal to God, who alone has it in his power to change her sex. What in the thirteenth century seemed like a mad wish for a Mosaic miracle, now only requires a good surgeon:

> You changed the staff to a snake before a million eyes,
> You Father in heaven, who did miracles for our ancestors with fire and
>   water,
> You changed the fire of the Chaldees so it would not burn hot,
> You changed Moses's hand to [leprous] white,

[Exodus 4:6: "Then the LORD said, 'Put your hand inside your cloak.' So Moses put his hand into his cloak, and when he took it out, it was leprous, like snow.... So Moses put his hand back into his cloak, and when he took it out, it was restored, like the rest of his flesh."]

> And the sea to dry land.
> In the desert you turned rock to water,
> Hard flint to a fountain.
> Who would then turn me from a man to woman?
> Were I only to have merited this, being so graced by your goodness.
> What shall I say? Why cry or be bitter?
> If my father in heaven has decreed upon me
> And has maimed me with an immutable deformity,

Here he's referring to his penis as a מום (*múm*), a "defect," a deformity.

> I do not wish to remove it.
> And the sorrow of the impossible
> Is a human pain that nothing will cure.

Kalonymus must find a way to live with the impossible wish. To bless what he would curse, because the tradition requires him to bless the bitter no less than the sweet:

> So I will bear and suffer
> Until I die and wither in the ground.
> And since I have learned from the tradition
> That we bless both the good and the bitter,
> I will bless in a voice, hushed and weak:
> Blessed are you, O Lord, our God,
> King of the Universe,
> Who has not made me a woman.[9]

Hushed and weak, with no answer to his prayers, cursed with this impossible pain of not being able to change his sex, he nevertheless utters the prayer all Orthodox Jewish men say to bless God for the blessing of their gender. To him it's no blessing, rather a curse. Yet he blesses God for the curse with which he's blessed because whatever comes from God is a blessing, even a curse. Would he ever have dreamed that seven hundred years later his impossible dream would have become a familiar reality for hundreds of thousands of transsexuals? Like Favorinus, his doubleness is gender-transgressive, but in the case of Kalonymus it is also a sacrilege, a scandalous violation of the covenant, of God's division of the sexes. Still today right-wing Christians [*and orthodox Jews*] rage at transsexuals who, defying the God-given division, insult God: they must be eradicated—by law. Ķalonymus defied two thousand years of male privilege to dream of being changed into a woman, dared to dream it aloud. In rhythmic Hebrew prose.

It's as if some doubleness in the air of Arles, this *urbs dupleix*, cleaves the genes of infant babies and promotes the birth of contradictory figures, citizens of enormous talent and accomplishment who fiercely hold together the double sides of their being: Celtic/Roman, Christian/pagan, Chiffonistes/Monnaidiers, royalists/revolutionaries. It can't be entirely an accident that Arles is the city in France with the highest proportion of twins born per capita.

In 1483, during a famine that led to desperation among farmers, shepherds in the hills, and some local people, the mob marched on the ghetto in the rue de la Juiverie, smashed walls, pillaged houses, and massacred men, women, and children. The people of the Church were complicit in the violence, inciting the mob, including the active participation of Franciscan friars and Carmelite monks, with crucifix in hand, exhorting the crowd to punish the treacherous race of God killers. The Church had reason to be pleased. The day after the riots, fifty Jews in Arles were converted.

In 1488 the Jews of Arles were expelled from the city and never returned. Those who agreed to convert were allowed to stay. The synagogue was destroyed, and soon there were no more Jews left in Arles.

Three hundred years later, in 1775, a decree of the parliament of Provence ordered certain Jews who had tried to reestablish themselves in Arles to leave within eight days. In 1773, and again in 1775, trading in Arles was forbidden to Jews by the parliament of Provence. After the French Revolution, some Jews from the Comtat Venaissin settled in Arles. There are a few Jews living in Arles today (including the town's only psychoanalyst), but no synagogue, no community center. Not surprisingly, neither are there any semiofficial gay bars in Arles; as Proust knew, Jews and homosexuals are often treated alike in Christian societies. The Municipal Museum possesses a rich collection of Jewish ritual objects and documents of the local Jews' long history.

I was shocked and surprised to learn that Jews were banned from living in Arles as recently as the eighteenth century. It took a revolution to finally end the power of a bigoted Church and a corrupt noble class. The revolutionary hero of Arles was Pierre-Antoine Antonelle, the city's first mayor. So I asked the Rock to tell me his story.

A Republic of Equals

The next day, the Rock began:

Antonelle is another of those contradictory, double personalities whose paradoxical existence reflects the doubleness of the city in which they were born. They called him—he even called himself—a "noble déclassé," an aristocrat who proudly, defiantly renounced his titles in order to embrace the revolutionary struggle of the people. His great biographer [*Pierre Serna*] called him oxymoronically an *aristocrate révolutionnaire*. Antoine d'Antonelle de Saint-Léger was born in Arles in 1747, the son of an extremely rich aristocratic family that had a *hôtel particulier* on the "wrong" side of town, down by the river where the workers, artisans, and boat people lived. The family titles dated only from the sixteenth century, when King Henry gaily knighted wealthy provincial bourgeois to acquire their resources for his armies. The older feudal families keenly despised such recently ennobled gentry. For the next couple of centuries, the men of the family abandoned the business of making war in favor of making and marrying money.

Antonelle's father died when his son was five years old; bereft of paternal influence, he grew up in Arles under the severe attention of his autocratic mother. Young Antonelle had nothing to say about his future. Since the death of his father, his mother had determined that he should have a military career. She saw in him a path to refurbishing the family's aristocratic pretensions by enrolling him in the king's army, as his ancestors had done long ago. She sent him off to a close family friend, Joseph-Amédée de Broglie, archbishop of Angoulême, to be groomed for a military career. The harsh rigidity of his education at the mercy of the archbishop's cruelty inspired Antonelle's life-long hatred of the clergy. At seventeen, he left for Paris, passed briefly through military school, then joined his regiment in Strasbourg.

When he returned to Paris, he harangued his mother for the gold he needed to support a life in which he spent more on six outfits, three thousand louis, than many nobles spent in a year. The archbishop complained to his mother about his gambling, his extravagance, and his debauchery, and that he avoided the company of honest women. He spent the next ten years leading a dissolute life in Paris, at enormous expense, occasionally attending court, where he had little success among the higher reaches of the aristocracy. Nothing was more withering than the arrogant superiority, the haughty morgue of the old feudal aristocrats at court toward nobles titled a mere two hundred years before. He found the military increasingly boring and unfulfilling. He discovered no charm in "commanding beggars" and "obeying fools." Toward the end of his service, his superiors complained that he spent all his time doing physics and mathematics. For reasons not entirely clear, he was denied the commission he had expected. At the age of thirty-five, disgusted with his career, bored with Paris, uninterested in the vanities of the court, he resigned from the military after seven years and returned to Arles. Escaping the constraints of military life, he wrote to his uncle, in the prolix style he favored, that he aspired "to the veritable happiness of living independent under a brilliant sky, in a delicious climate, in the midst of a green, perfumed, flowered countryside—land that is charming and fertile, watered by the healthful waters of a superb river, planted with fig trees and olives, covered with numerous flocks, enriched with crops and vineyards and meadows."[1] He became a sort of hermit, burying himself in the family mansion on the rue de la Roquette—formerly called the rue de la Monnaie—on the other side of town from where for centuries the nobility mostly lived, up here on me, on L'Hauture.

Abandoning his military career marked a rupture with his past and his milieu. At thirty-five, he had accomplished nothing. He decided to catch up on the education he never had and set about reading the philosophers of the Enlightenment, who were his contemporaries.

He never married or showed any interest in preserving the name of the family d'Antonelle. Sexually, he was, how do you say? kinky (*pervers*). He wrote long, imploring letters to his fiancée begging her to slap him around:

"You'll never know," he wrote to her, "how happy I am under your blows. And especially how happy I could become if you beat me furiously, and here I beg you take me literally. I would passionately love to be slapped, punished, bruised by your hand, which could wound me mortally if you wanted. . . . What would it be if you deigned to really bear down, let loose multiple slaps as hard as you could, slaps of fury, hitting and hitting again without pity the happy madman, the idolizing lover of so much barbarity [*l'idolâtre amateur de tant de barbarie*], eternalizing this unequal struggle in which it would be so sweet for me to feel constantly beaten and crushed?"[2]

Is he not nuts, this happy madman? "The idolizing lover of so much barbarity"? What does that even mean? Performatively, what is he trying to do? He seems to think that if he utterly abases himself before her, as if she were a fetish (in the sense of some idolatrous object of worship), this cruel goddess will give him relief at last from . . . from what? From some great guilt, some crime of being? Maybe he's right about the goddess; maybe she will at last give him what he wants. Suppose he somehow knew she was a sadist and that this would appeal to her. Perhaps, if she were in fact a sadist, she wouldn't give him what he exactly wants so badly.

Observe, by the way, that he has nothing to say about her. Like the lady, *la domna* of troubadour poets, she is all but invisible in this poem. She is elevated to such idolized superiority that she all but vanishes—so exalted that she can conveniently become the merest pretext for the poet to speak of his distress. I said a poem, but this, of course, is a letter he writes to her, in a poetic style whose abrupt, compulsive rhythm mimes the masochistic slaps he craves. I note that the phrase *"l'idolâtre amateur de tant de barbarie"* is a perfect alexandrine, the twelve-syllable form of classical French verse. It's rather beautiful in a scary way.

It's clear he's not in love so much with her as with her ferocity, brutality, cruelty. He takes exquisite pleasure in enumerating all the levels of pain he dreams of welcoming from her hand. It excites him to imagine the forms of beastliness he lends her, as if her sadistic impulses corresponded exactly with what his masochism desires. In his imagination, he is enacting her cruelty, the barbarity he wants her to execute. He becomes like Baudelaire's "Héautontimouromenos," the self-tormenter who beats himself "without anger and without hate, like a butcher."[3] He is his own torturer, simultaneously sadist and masochist, the double-sided nature of his perversion.

The scary part is that the barbarity he so poetically idolizes becomes, seven years later, a terrifying reality. He is one of those, at the behest of Robespierre, who conducts the Terror, a leader of the jury that during the revolution condemned hundreds—no, thousands—across France to the guillotine, brutally, mechanically, without hatred or anger, like butchers.

Let me resume a little. After quitting the military, Antonelle lived down by the river among artisans and sailors who were much more attuned to the discontent and revolutionary ideas circulating up and down the valley of the Rhône. It was a quartier whose inhabitants, more turbulent, more open to Marseille and the culture of the river, were very different from the conservative agricultural workers and the hidebound aristocrats and professional types, doctors, lawyers, officials, who resisted change. He surrounded himself with books from Nîmes that he couldn't find in royalist Arles, where, when he asked to order copies of the Bible and the Great Encyclopedia, the bookseller refused, saying he was "too good a Catholic to distribute these two impious books." Arles was a little island of obscurantism amid a Provence largely open to philosophical debates, literary culture, and science.

Antonelle undertook a rigorous course of self-study that centered on reading the leading figures of the Enlightenment, particularly Voltaire, Condorcet, Montesquieu, Condillac, and Rousseau, but also the more radical political thought of Locke and Hobbes. In isolation he developed a meticulous and far-ranging critique of the French monarchy and its institutions, while he embraced ideals and values that were its strict opposite. Beginning with an intense study of history and of political science, Antonelle created for himself a philosophical position that separated him from his caste and declassed him from all aristocratic pretensions to distinction:

> When someone tells me that a man is just, wise, courageous, prudent, humane, virtuous, that he has talent, knowledge, genius, those are words that have meaning, words that can't fail to matter to me; but when someone tells me that a man is noble, or a commoner, a marquis or count, I understand nothing and I take no more interest in these beautiful ideas than in any other fiction of the mind.[4]

And again, he writes:

> Nobility rests on theft, defended in every age by a new generation of thieves. There is no biological determinism, no distinctive racial sign, but only a complicity that's fraudulently hereditary. Nobles are skillful bandits,

treating their brothers as a beast of burden, implementing slavery and iniquity into law, which then become an immutable and sacred code that other bandits must forever protect and before whom human rights disappear.[5]

Antonelle writes as he reads, disputing, concurring, arguing with himself the virtues of different political systems. He writes on the reform of the monarchy, with reflections on legitimist struggles against all forms of despotism. That in turn leads him to consider religion, which he denounces not only for its ecclesiastical institutions but its dogmas of faith:

> What do I see in history? What one sees on the stage [*scène*] of the world: the tyranny of the strong, the oppression of the weak, the success of the skillful con man or the lucky scoundrel, the vices and misfortune of all. The unique obligation of man is probity, just as his true glory is virtue. The rest is only childish babble, prejudice, shadow plays. Justice and goodness. That's the pure gold. Nothing is truly valuable except what they produce by their diversity.[6]

He proposes a philosophy of tolerance in which the nation is strengthened by its collective diversity, a "harmonious plurality." He advances a notion of individualism in which all are free to pursue their own forms of happiness, as far as their freedom doesn't impinge on the space of someone else. The most intensely personal acts are constrained only by society's judgment of what is reasonable and what is in the interest of good order and the well-being of all. He proposes an idea of tolerance in which the exercise of every form of personal liberty is authorized within a social order that aims for the greatest common happiness. Not being content to elaborate a theory of the just and good society, he puts its principle to work in his own relations with his tenants, granting them time to reimburse their debts, or letting them expire.

Antonelle developed a psychological theory that begins with the notion that man is an inexplicable enigma. Man doesn't know at all what he is, what he was, what he will become: all the movements of his body, all the feelings of his soul, everything that makes him capable of thinking, of speaking and doing, belong to a mechanism of which he will never have the secret. He is an inexplicable enigma to himself. He is ignorant of himself in all the moments of his existence. He doesn't understand the first principle, the means, or the end.

Antonelle extols "*le peuple*" and the working class. His most impassioned arguments are reserved for the condition of women. He understood that the greatest obstacle to general equality was the submission of women. Equality begins with their liberation. About the condition of women, he wrote: "Unjust laws weigh on the two sexes with a revolting inequality directed against the weakest and the least guilty."[7] His revulsion at the inequality of women may have been the first sign of a political, not to say revolutionary, awakening.

Most of his energy went to excoriating the clergy. A confirmed atheist, he thought that too many ecclesiastics adopted their clerical dress for the prestige of its appearance, for the credit it received and the respect it elicited—not to mention the wealth and power it brought:

The whole system of faith rests on the construction of a false perception of reality, a perception that is then substituted for a true reality, and what is worst, it becomes the only reality. That is the dangerous usurpation. It is a transvestitism not only of the body by priestly clothes, but of reason dressed in chimera. That's the madness of religion. It prevents a real and direct relation to knowledge and to the world. It distances people from themselves like madness.[8]

To the "fanaticism of religion" he opposed tolerance and forbearance. He defended Jews and Protestants not because of their views but because of the abuse they had suffered. To the inequality of the monarchic system, with its rigid hierarchies, he proposed a healthy system of equality based on the value and virtue of people's work.

He was contemptuous of ordinary conventions of dress. He wrote to his mother:

Speaking only . . . of the intolerable tyranny of that childishness we call manners and fashion, I've still not found anyone who has had the boldness to dress uniquely according to his own taste. [*Pour ne parler ici que d'une vraie puerilité qui, par l'importance que l'esprit d'imitation lui donne, fera mieux ressortir l'insoutenable tyrannie de cet enfantillage que nous appelons usage et modes, je n'ai trouvé encore personne qui eût l'intrépidité de s'habiller uniquement à son gout.*][9]

His own taste was appalling. He was *débraillé*, as the French say, disheveled, unkempt, scruffy, *déguenillé*, dressed in rags and tatters. His negligence was a stain on Arles high society and was remarked upon in Paris. It was a way of excluding himself from aristocratic values, a visible gesture to mark his *déclassement nobiliaire*.

After quitting the army, he spent six years in virtual isolation, reading philosophy and meditating on the nature of government; he defined for himself a radically new legitimacy, no longer based on inheritance, on wealth or title or distinction, but on reason and science. His work on himself, by himself, led inevitably to political engagement. In 1788, at his own expense he published anonymously *The Catechism of the Third Estate* for the use of all the provinces of France and especially Provence, in which he fiercely defends the demand of the third estate to enlarge its representation in the National Assembly in order to be superior to that of the other two estates, and to distribute the tax burden equally among all the members of society. He deplored that the fiefs of nobles, inherited with their titles, were exempt from paying taxes, as if the land weren't part of the nation, as if it belonged to a foreign government. The *Cathechism* had a certain success and was twice reedited.

In January 1789 Antonelle became more directly involved in local politics and in the pamphlet war waged between aristocrats demanding that their privileges be respected and the increasingly assertive third estate demanding their elimination. Its greatest champion in Provence was Count Mirabeau, the fulminating orator and political moderate, who became the model for Antonelle of an aristocrat *déclassé*. He followed closely the events in Aix, where Count Mirabeau had come to vote with the nobles in the provincial assembly. The nobles refused to seat him, so he postulated for the third estate, and they accepted him. In January, Antonelle insists that Mirabeau is "vicious and mean [*méchant*], consumed by self-love and devouring ambition," "with fire in his head, violence in his humors, and a frenzy in his soul that is exclusive of any justice or moderation." Later in the year, as Mirabeau succeeds more and more in advancing the revolutionary agenda, Antonelle alters his opinion of the fiery count. "Is it possible," he asks, "that a soul as corrupt as he could have the glory of alone being charged with having justly embraced the defense of the good cause?" Still later in the year he is utterly seduced by this "wise man and little hero." "Look at what he did and said, at what he wants someday to say and do, and tell me if anyone can act better or better speak."[10] Mirabeau was elected to the Estates General that convened in May. He left Aix for Paris, where he became a major figure in the subsequent National Constituent Assembly.

Antonelle pursued an increasingly public role in Arles as an eloquent and enlightened defender of the third estate, to the dismay and anger of his aristocratic peers up here on *L'Hauture*. The month of July 1789 was when everything changed for France and for Antonelle. On the fourteenth the people of Paris tore down the Bastille, the hulking prison, symbol of arbitrary royal power. Three days later the king went in public with a *cocarde* in his hat, the blue-white-and-red ribbon that signified allegiance not to him but to the nation.

In Arles, on July 25, seventy-eight people signed a text, a patriotic decree that advanced the cause of the third estate against the claims of the aristocrats. The artisan corporations objected that most of the signers belonged to what they called the "high third," bourgeois and professionals. Artisans and sailors, who felt excluded, went to Antonelle to solicit his opinion on whether they should sign. It was the first occasion for Antonelle, the aristocratic hermit, to emerge from his anonymity in a document that earnestly exhorted the artisans and sailors to sign the decree. That he was consulted by them indicates that the most radical forces in the city looked to him for guidance and wisdom.

I remember the day in August 1781 when the *tocsin* began ringing furiously. The rapid pealing, a hundred times a minute, distinguishes the tocsin from the funereal *glas*, which tolls very slowly [*fifteen times a minute*]. The tocsin was rung whenever there was some imminent danger, a fire, an invasion, a shipwreck, or whenever the population was called to assemble in case of some urgency. That day, rumors had swept through town that the king and his aristocrats had hired gangs of brigands to destroy the peasants' crops or their property, as a means of imposing political control.

Panic spread, and the peasants took up arms against the brigands who were said to be burning barns and razing crops. The peasants were half-crazed, suffering not only from drought, from bitter winters and terrible harvests in 1788 and 1789, but also from ergotism. It is a malady, often fatal, that comes from eating a fungus, ergot, that grows on rye grain under conditions such as those disastrous ones (dry, cold winter, rain-soaked summer) that afflicted France that year. Peasants who had meager harvests were reduced to eating the fungus-infected rye that in good years they would normally discard. Ergot contains a chemical called ergotamine, which is used to make lysergic acid—not LSD itself, but one of the precursor chemicals, which can have similar hallucinogenic effects.

Thinking that the brigands were in the pay of aristocrats seeking revenge for the revolution, the armed peasants began attacking manor houses belonging to the nobles. During the attacks on the estates of the feudal nobility and on convents, their main objective was reported to have been finding and destroying the documents granting lords their feudal privileges over the peasantry. In some cases, the manor houses were burned along with the documents. Hundreds of manor houses are reported to have been burned this way.

Even though Antonelle discounted the panic—he called it a "puerile alarm"—nevertheless he agreed to serve as one of the commanders of the local militia

IX.1. Hôtel de Ville, built in the Reign of Louis XIV

formed to confront the invaders. He had, after all, been in the king's army for ten years. He was the only commander who supported the demands of the artisans, the sailors, and their corporations.

On December 14, 1789, the National Assembly, with the approval of the king, issued a decree that abolished all the municipal governments in France and ordered new elections. It changed the title of the chief magistrate from consul to mayor. Most remarkably, it established the right of every citizen to be nominated to municipal office. For five centuries, Arles had been exclusively ruled by the Church, by its aristocrats, and by the very rich. This time, people freely elected a slate of the third estate that included a shoemaker, a carpenter, a peasant, two lawyers, a merchant, a doctor, an officer of the court, and one declassed aristocrat, sympathetic to the artisans: our man Antonelle, who was elected mayor. He swore "to maintain with all his power the Constitution of the kingdom, to be faithful to the Nation, to the law, to the king, and to well perform his function."

I've told you that the *hôtel particulier* belonging to the family d'Antonelle stood on the other side of town from me, on the principal street that led from the center of town to the river, the *rue de la Monnaie* (now the *rue de la Roquette*). The revolutionary circle of artisans and sailors, merchants, and professionals who met there called itself La Monnaye and its citizens *monnaidiers*. The aristocratic circle that ruled Arles, and their conservative allies among the farmworkers, called themselves La Chiffone and its adherents *chiffonistes*, from the name of the house of the late *abbé* Chiffon, where the first meetings took place. The geographical division of the city—upper l'Hauture/lower la Roquette—emblematized the revolutionary struggle of royalists versus Jacobins. The division in Arles between chiffonistes and monnaidiers was constantly cited in Paris and became a microcosm, a model, or a metaphor for the revolutionary struggle itself.

Antonelle as mayor makes his mark on the city and introduces the revolution by enacting the first decrees and laws of the Constituent Assembly. He defends the third estate, the poor, the nation against the privileged. He orders the brothers of the Christian schools to make their students copy and learn "The Declaration of the Rights of Man." He was not aiming to promote the identity of Arles but to allow its students to be recognized as belonging to the French nation, abandoning local particularities in favor of nationality perceived as a transcendent social pact. Politically, there is a reform of the police. The people, now in control, organize a national guard as well as a new system of justice, with the installation of a new set of judges.

Arles was beginning a third very bitter winter of poverty and misery. There were spring freezes in 1789–1790. In November 1790, after diluvian rains, the Rhône overflowed, and not for the first (or last time) the citizens of Arles sought refuge on me, and the pious asked for help from above. As Antonelle wrote sarcastically, "Those who recognize divine causes in the effects of Nature see the finger of God in this great calamity. And so, after men had befouled the earth with all sorts of crimes, the author of nature submerged it to purify it."[11] The city asked for help from the state.

In December 1790 the city celebrated the new order, and Antonelle made a speech denouncing the old regime and praising the new government.

On September 28, 1791, the king issued a declaration accepting the constitution proposed by the assembly. He declared:

> To all Citizens, *Salut*. I have accepted the Constitution and I will use all my efforts to maintain it and to see to its execution. The end of the revolution has arrived, and it is time that the reestablishing of order serves to give to the Constitution the support that it most requires; it is time to fix the

opinion of Europe on the destiny of France and to show that the French are worthy of being free.[12]

The king wished to believe that a corner had been turned and that the revolution had reached its term. In fact, it was only the end of the beginning. His own execution, the promulgation of two more constitutions, and bloody terror would be required before the end finally came.

Many of the most prominent nobles fled the city. In 1791 the council of Arles decided unanimously to destroy the coats of arms on the houses of the aristocracy ("standards of haughty pride that wound reason") rather than simply plastering them over. They banned insulting differences in funerals. At the cemetery they ordered that everyone should have the same cross, the same number of priests and even ornaments. In 1740 the artisans had been excluded from the government of the city by the nobles; now the artisans in control aimed to wipe away the whole aristocratic past.

Arles became a privileged space for the confrontation between the sides in the revolution. It had patriots who were fleeing Catholic repression in the Comtat, and Catholics from Nîmes suffering from Protestant reprisals. It's the religion question that sharpens the opposition between Arles *la rouge* and Arles *la blanche*. Antonelle, as we have seen, was fiercely anticlerical. His hatred and contempt for religion were so deeply rooted that every Friday, when Catholics forswear meat, he would order an enormous headcheese [*tête de veau*] from a charcuterie in Nîmes and would eat it ostentatiously with his friends.

He had a fierce adversary in the archbishop of Arles, Monseigneur du Lau, rich and powerful, with resources extending beyond the city. The archbishop became the leader of those in Arles who viewed with horror the revolutionary reforms, who dreamed of the old order and eventually became counterrevolutionaries. At a moment when the clergy was under pressure to swear an oath of fidelity to the constitution, Monseigneur Lau took the occasion to publish an apostolic letter in which the pope denounced the Enlightenment principles that inspired the civil constitution of the clergy. In response, Antonelle personally attacked the prelate, calling him "a false prophet . . . who has come to teach us that if the nation doesn't continue to lodge him in a beautiful palace, to gratify him with an income of 100,000 *livres*, to allow him to exercise in the Midi of France the immediate jurisdiction he received from heaven (for those are his own words), why then the realm of moral consciousness (*l'empire de la conscience*) will be shaken to its foundation."[13] Like most of the clergy, Lau refused the Civil Constitution of the clergy in 1790. He polemicized with

Antonelle, who freely expressed his anticlericalism. Lau was assassinated in 1792 in the Church of the Carmelites in Paris, which had become an improvised prison for counterrevolutionary priests. Antonelle worked to counter the power of religious dogmas over the popular will in the city known for its bigotry. In 1790 the National Assembly abolished monastic orders and suppressed many archbishoprics.

The opponents of the revolution founded a society and proclaimed the duties of a true Frenchman to be submission of all to the orders of the king, the return of traditional forms of religion, and the rejection of revolutionary ideas and feelings. A little later, those around Antonelle organized the Society of Friends of the Constitution and elected him its first president. The society affiliated itself with the Jacobin Club in Paris and those organizations in Marseille, Nîmes, Aix, Montpellier, and Avignon. The revolution so profoundly marked families in Arles that they maintained their political orientation well into the next century. It's been said that a republican family never became royalist; the descendants of royalists hardly ever changed their politics.

The violence perpetrated against nuns and young women who refused to recognize the civil constitution of the clergy, as well as the expulsion of priests from Arles and those ecclesiastics who had fled from Nîmes, exacerbated tensions in the city and fanned the hatred between the two sides. Nevertheless, Antonelle was remarkably successful in bringing revolutionary ideas and practices to this deeply conservative city. He had such widespread local support that they renamed *la place de l'Hôtel de Ville*, the great central square, *la place Antonelle*. His success led him to misjudge the depth of his support, and the necessity of his presence to command it, which led him to make a fatal error of political judgment. He abandoned Arles to fight on the side of the revolutionaries in Avignon who were struggling to overcome the papist government that had controlled the city and its region since the fourteenth century. The revolutionaries in Avignon wanted to send representatives to the General Assembly in Paris to join the French nation as a fully secularized, intrinsic part of France. His departure destabilized the balance of power in Arles and allowed the chiffonistes to take control of the city council. The city was in chaos.

After a few weeks, Antonelle chose to return to Aix to persuade his allies in the Provençal assembly to send troops to disarm the chiffonistes. Before leaving the city, he praised the liberating army of Marseille and exhorted his followers in the most exalted terms to hold firm against the reactionaries: the young monnaidiers greeted him with cries in the street: "Vive la nation! Vive Antonelle! Et merde au roi!"

In 1790, he stopped signing himself as "Chevalier d'Antonelle" or even "D'Antonelle, cadet [*the younger*]"; he dropped the particle and signed "Pierre-Antoine Antonelle."

In Aix, on August 30, 1791, he was elected by the Provincial Assembly to represent the local Jacobins at the Legislative Assembly in Paris. He took with him a reputation as a transformative, revolutionary mayor; a soldier; a brilliant, pitiless polemicist; a serious political thinker; and a fine analyst of politics with a passionate detestation of all hierarchy and inequality.

Already a founding member in Arles of the new revolutionary party, Antonelle was promoted in Paris by Robespierre to be the president of the Jacobins. He performed several important missions for the party, then was promoted to the revolutionary tribunal, charged with judging those accused of being enemies of the revolution. Like Mirabeau, *un aristocrate déclassé*, but more radically bloody minded, he was one of the *implacables* on the revolutionary tribunal, one of those pitiless jurors who had no mercy, who rabidly pronounced sentences of death. He was foreman of the jury that tried and condemned Marie-Antoinette. He was probably complicit in the cruelty with which she was treated awaiting trial in a dank cell below the courtyard of the Conciergerie, slimy with water seeping in from the nearby Seine. With some reservations, he later served on the jury that massively condemned the former allies of the Jacobins, the moderate Girondins. On a day when his jury condemned thirty-one Girondins to the guillotine, he dined with his bloody-minded peers on a fine fat hen while heads fell. One of his Jacobin rivals at the time judged him to be "too dissipated, too gourmand, too given over to the gross orgies of the Palais Royal to be able to think of anything else."

Phillipe d'Orleans, a cousin of the king, had revolutionary sympathies, so when he inherited the Palais Royal, he renamed its great central garden "*le jardin de la Révolution*." He transformed it into a little city within the city from which the police were banned. Short of cash, he turned it into a moneymaking—how to call it?—mall. He restored and enlarged it and made it available for furious political debates. He installed 145 boutiques under its arcades—fashion shops, perfumers, bookstores, sellers of stamps and engraving, music boxes, old coins. Some of them may still be there. Along with denizens of its cafés and seekers of entertainment, it attracted a raffish crowd of gamblers, prostitutes, and flaneurs. Besides being an authentic revolutionary of the highest ideals, a fighter for the possibility of a truly representative democracy, Antonelle was also a whore hound. He would rather pay for sex than get it free from a woman who loved him. We know that his mentor, the abbé, told his mother that even as a young man he had no interest in honest women. The Palais Royal was where he dissipated his seemingly inexhaustible energy, probably under the sting of whips.

By accepting the fiction of a massive conspiracy, the Jacobin juries daily, with mechanical efficiency, ordered the death of anyone faintly perceived to be an enemy of the revolution, even among their closest allies; they massacred the moderate revolutionaries, the Girondins, for not being murderous enough. They sent them all to the guillotine, "without hatred and without anger," and so invented the industrial style of bureaucratic murder. It often sufficed merely to be accused to be guillotined. At the end of the Terror, defendants before the court were granted neither the right to call witnesses nor to mount a defense. There was no appeal. The whole procedure was reduced to the indictment and the judgment. Eighteen thousand people were sent to the guillotine by revolutionary tribunals in Paris and around the country. At the frenetic height of its operations, the revolutionary tribunal in Paris, on which Antonelle was a juror, was sentencing eight hundred people per month to the guillotine—twenty-six per day.

Antonelle was the first to be named by Robespierre to sit on the revolutionary tribunal, and for a while he was its leader. He must have been judged to be one of the *pur et dur*, a fervent hard-liner who could be counted on to enforce the Terror without hesitation. He sat from October 1793 to February 1794, and during that time, in the trials on which he served, the juries ordered two deportations, three prison sentences, ten acquittals, and the death penalty thirty-eight times—71 percent of the time. He served on fewer juries than some because he was chosen for the longest and most important ones: the trial of Marie-Antoinette, and that of his former revolutionary companions, the Girondins. Antonelle was seen as the most influential juror, whose judgments generally determined those of the others; both trials ended in death for all the defendants. At the trial of a noble revolutionary, as the defense seemed about to win and the accused rushed to embrace his lawyers, Antonelle arose to denounce the aristocracy and the counterrevolutionary intentions of the defendant. People in the court cheered; the jury bowed to popular will and sent him to the guillotine.

Many critics of Antonelle have seen the exercise of his intransigent cruelty as a way of taking revenge on his hated aristocratic identity. He was not a cruel man, by all accounts; he treated his workers fairly and saw to their old age. He was much beloved in Arles, and when he died, there was a great outpouring. However, there must have been a moment when his self-torturing desires to be beaten and punished revealed their sadistic component. Perhaps only a masochist of such extreme perversity could become the agent of such monstrous cruelty administered on a vast scale, condemning hundreds to die with little or no justification. Perhaps I'm wrong to judge his work on the revolutionary tribunal as if it reflected some psychological motive. Maybe he was just a banal cog in the political machine of the Terror, acting under the dictatorial orders of Robespierre, with the beneficent efficiency of Dr. Guillotine's invention (no more drunken executioners).

During the trial of the Girondins, Antonelle had a public moment of hesitancy about rushing to judge them, his old companions in arms. That was enough to arouse the suspicions of the hard-liners—doubts about his revolutionary fervor that were sharpened when he began to publish his "Motivations." He was the only one of the jurors who thought they had a responsibility to the idea of the revolution to be transparent, to explain the reasons and allege the factual bases of their mostly deadly judgments. He felt called to transparency. The revolution must also be a revolution in how officials address the public. Things must be said, aloud, not hidden. His "Motivations" also had the didactic function of instructing the people in the theory and principles of revolutionary transformation.

Robespierre found that these public justifications of the court's decisions opened it unnecessarily to more scrutiny and criticism, and he had no patience for Antonelle's long-winded defenses:

> For some time, juries have introduced the practice of motivating their individual opinions to the audience of the Revolutionary Tribunal with the resulting inconveniences. Considering as well that it is contrary to the spirit of this institution that the members of the jury transform themselves into orators.... The [Committee of Public Safety] reminds them that juries must be content to give their declarations purely and simply, in conformity with principles and laws without lending themselves to discussions.[14]

Antonelle was forever lending himself to discussions. He was given to speaking on all occasions, eternally, in long, complexly structured sentences expounding his political theories and examining opinions. He has a similarly prolix style of writing:

> The pilot of public safety [*Robespierre*], captaining the great ship in the midst of so many dangerous reefs, beaten by the waves of a tumultuous sea, with a crew that's half mutinied, under fire from thirty pirates, must not

be compared to that sort of pilot, who, conducting the ship over its accustomed waves, assisted by a united and docile crew, holds an easy rudder, without having to harden his grip. It follows that the French people were obliged to be violent in order not to become slaves.[15]

Antonelle could never shut up if he had an audience. In prison he exasperated his revolutionary comrades, victims like him of Robespierre, by expounding nonstop on the principles of revolutionary justice with an aristocratic nonchalance, a casual politeness that clashed with the bloody Jacobin extremism of his rhetoric.

His enemies claimed that he incurred the wrath of Robespierre because he was too bold, too radical, too ready to accept the angry demands of the people to condemn the accused to the guillotine. Others want to believe that his compulsive talking, his endless justifications for his decisions as a juror, was a mask that revealed his true humanity, and betrayed his silent opposition to Robespierre.

As a result of suspicions he aroused, Antonelle would have been executed but for the Thermidor Reaction, when the Jacobin enemies of Robespierre first arrested him, then tried him, and promptly guillotined him.

The fall of the dictator was celebrated in Arles during the revolution, as it was on all important occasions, by bull games that were held in the great central square, *la place du Marché* [*now the place de la République*]. Bleachers were set up along the walls, and people crammed into the archbishop's residence overlooking the square for the best view. Several amateurs at the games received serious wounds, and three died. One bull that had been tormented to a furious rage chased some spectators upstairs into the residence and reached the second floor, packed with people. If they hadn't been able to shut him up in the vestibule, he would have thrown a great number of spectators from the balcony or out the windows.

Aristocratic republicans and rich bourgeois, many of whom had made a fortune in acquiring the confiscated property of exiled aristocrats, launched a murderous hunt of Jacobins and others who had supported the radical popular uprising [*particularly the proletarian sans-culottes, who preferred pants to aristocratic breeches*] and who had applauded the reign of terror conducted by Robespierre's murderous Committee of Public Safety.

Because he had been imprisoned by Robespierre, Antonelle escaped the White Terror, the furious reaction against the revolutionary Jacobins that followed the death of the Incorruptible Tyrant. Antonelle was saved by his prison, another very *felix carcar*. Now he was free, but dangerously vulnerable to being remembered as the uncompromising militant radical he recently used to be.

Antonelle lay very low, then began to support with his journalism the democratic forces that resisted the reactionary White Terror. When an armed mob of young royalists, the so-called golden youth, threatened the government, it called on a young general, Napoleon Buonaparte, to disperse the mob with a "whiff of grapeshot." Antonelle allied himself with the republican government that emerged from the Thermidor Reaction, whose executive declared itself to be a new five-member Directoire, composed mainly of wealthy republican aristocrats. They had written and had voted into law a new constitution with census suffrage. Only men, older than twenty-one, who could read and paid taxes, could vote. A mere thirty thousand met the further requirement that to vote, one had to be a property owner.

Secretly, Antonelle joined with other radical Jacobins in a clandestine conspiracy to overthrow the Directoire and install what Antonelle called, perhaps for the first time in history, "Representative democracy—a republic of equality, one and indivisible." He wrote, brilliantly:

> Unless you consider that the People are destined only to believe, to obey, to work and to pay, the true order in a democratic republic must be founded on equality made possible within direct voting assemblies, which are not distorted and not diminished, to which all citizens would continue to be admitted in order to choose their representatives, without having to present a certificate of literacy, or the witness of two property owners. . . . Any political system based on the distinction of a disqualifying difference is therefore inherently aristocratic.[16]

Write that down in capital letters:

ANY POLITICAL SYSTEM BASED ON THE DISTINCTION OF A DISQUALIFYING DIFFERENCE IS THEREFORE INHERENTLY ARISTOCRATIC.

At first, it might seem implausible that Antonelle, one of the most sanguinary Jacobins during the revolution, could be among the first to advocate for representative democracy, anticipating twentieth-century politics when women and Blacks demanded the vote. Women in France didn't get it until 1944. In the eyes of Antonelle, the Directoire, the new government, was already on the way to becoming what he feared most, an oligarchy, a republic of aristocrats—educated property owners who rule:

In the name of democracy, out of respect for the rights of man, for the common good, one cannot exclude women or the poor or the ignorant, the perverse, the stupid, or those who oppose the government. Otherwise, there can be no true democracy, only a veiled aristocracy, in a system based on the distinction of a disqualifying difference.[17]

It was his obsession with equity, with radical equality, that drove his political passion and progressively led him to believe that only a bloody revolution would eliminate the Old Regime. The nobility could not be managed; it had to be overthrown.

After the Terror, when the revolution had succeeded in eliminating the aristocratic class, he worked with Gracchus Babeuf on the radical journal *Le Tribun du Peuple*. Babeuf was a revolutionary socialist with ideas of abolishing private property that anticipated Marx. Antonelle joined his secret conspiracy to incite an uprising against the government of the Directoire. The plot was uncovered, Babeuf was tried and executed, and Antonelle was briefly imprisoned—again.

From then on, Antonelle worked and wrote in favor of installing representative democracy until 1799, when, on the 18 Brumaire, Napoleon's coup d'état put an end to public advocacy. It seems too obvious to assume that his passion for political equality arose from his masochistic self-hatred and his wish to punish the regime that gave him his privilege, titles, and wealth. Maybe his politics were revenge directed at his autocratic mother, who had groomed him to be a knight in the king's army. But before psychologizing, listen to his voice in his "Manifesto of Equals" of 1796, published after the death of Robespierre:

We need not only that equality of rights written into the Declaration of the Rights of Man and Citizen; we want it in our midst, under the roofs of our houses. . . . Let it at last end, this great scandal that our descendants will never believe existed! Disappear at last, revolting distinctions between rich and poor, great and small, masters and servants, rulers and ruled. . . . The moment has come to found the REPUBLIC OF EQUALS, the great home open to all. . . . The organization of real equality, the only one that responds to all needs, without causing any victims, without costing any sacrifice, will not at first please everyone. The selfish, the ambitious, will tremble with rage.[18]

For all his utopian dreams, Antonelle had no illusions about the inevitability of resistance to a regime of equality. He knew how things worked in Arles.

Every action generated a raging reaction. Two sides, separated by only a few blocks, saw epic bloody battles between chiffonistes and monnaidiers—L'Hauture on high and La Roquette down below, aristocrats and sans-culottes. Antonelle knew that despite all the advantages of true representative democracy, it would not fail to arouse the rage of the other side, selfish and ambitious. The inveterate doubleness of Arles led it to a model of political life that looks a lot like what the United States has become: a sort of permanent civil war between two sides that hate each other, locked in an implacable struggle, sharing the same space. In Arles, the disqualifying difference was class; in America today, it's the color of your skin. For Antonelle, a truly democratic regime must rest on three fundamental rights: the right of universal suffrage, the right of peaceful assembly, and the right to resist oppression. Reduced to its essentials, representative democracy is the right to vote and the right to education.

He defined the theory of the alternation of governing political parties, founded on elections organized with universal suffrage. Only education, proceeding slowly, a process of civic apprenticeship spread out over time, is the just guarantee of the right to vote, while the citizen learns through elections to recognize the legitimacy of the regime.

And again:

Everything works to serve the dominant class, boudoirs, salons, betting parlors (*tripots*) and colleges, cafés and schools, balls, holidays, spectacles, long walks, whores, restaurant owners, big and little things, good institutions and bad ones, everything works to profit the dominant class, even certain rights, the most legitimate, the most sacred, like freedom of press.... Yes, in the disastrous state of inequality in which we are wasting away, everything favors and enhances the very few, everything weighs on the great mass of working, useful people.[19]

When Napoleon came to power in 1799, Antonelle was sent briefly into exile in Italy. After a few years he returned to Arles, where he lived peacefully until his death on his considerable family fortune, a large part of which he devoted to helping the unfortunate.

His funeral was a scandal. The mayor of Arles, Perrin de Jonquières, reported to the prefect the outrage at his burial:

I wasn't a little surprised when I saw the priest appear to announce that M. d'Antonelle, having lived and died a philosopher [*i.e., no Christian*], ought not to receive funeral honors. No priest willing to collect the body, it was escorted to the cemetery by officials from the various charities he had so beneficently endowed. The most admired citizens of Arles assembled at Antonelle's *hôtel particulier* to compose the funeral procession. As soon as his body appeared in the street, the bells of Saint-Césaire began to toll, but they were quickly silenced. A general cry went up, "What! There's only one priest? Is that how they treat the father of the poor?" Many of the poor, tears in their eyes, deploring the loss of their benefactor and begging the misericord of heaven on his behalf, contrasted sharply with the silence of the priest, who, contrary to the usual practice, was muttering a prayer one couldn't hear. Once we arrived at the church, an even more scandalous scene awaited us, not a candle was lit on the altar or elsewhere. The body had been disposed down from the church. The agitation of the crowd was at its height. At every moment I was afraid of an explosion on the part of the assembled people indignant at these proceedings. We went to the edge of the grave, the priest whispered the absolution, sprinkled holy water, and made no funeral oration.[20]

In the end, Antonelle had the last word. His death marked the beginning of the end of the Church's role in dominating life in Arles.

Antonelle died in 1817, about the time when Arles started to fall as far as it could go. Terrible floods during the Napoleonic years devastated the city. There were six or seven until the mammoth one in 1856 that turned Arles into Venice. The emperor himself came to inspect the loss. Only the nobles living on me were spared widespread destruction.

For most of the last fifteen hundred years, Arles had been a farm town whose farmers lived for protection on the east side near their land, while the boatmen lived near the river on the west. By 1850, the farmers had moved out of the city and taken up residence on their lands, and the boatmen had disappeared, replaced by the railroad. By the end of the century, Arles had become a proto-industrial city that employed people mostly at work on fixing trains in the *atelier* near the Alyscamps. Or they were employed in the saltworks on the shore, dredging salt for brine to mix with the abundant local limestone to produce an indispensable alkali—bicarbonate of soda, i.e., soda ash—to supply the soap factories in Marseille. Arles was barely getting along until, in the twentieth century, things got worse: two world wars occurred, the city was badly bombed as the Germans retreated, the railyard atelier shut down, salt began to come more cheaply from mines, and the biscuit factory that had employed a lot of women left town. By 2000, Arles was said by some to be the poorest city in France.

Not anymore! You won't believe this. In the thirteenth year of the new millennium, Tuché, the goddess of fortune, turned her smile on Arles. After hitting rock bottom (excuse the pun), a perfect miracle occurred—not for the first time in the history of Arles, as we've seen. The city received the direct infusion of hundreds of millions of euros from the LUMA Foundation, whose founders, Maja Hoffmann and her father, Luc, heirs to the Swiss pharmaceutical fortune of Hoffmann-La Roche, loved the city and sometimes lived in the Camargue. They acquired the abandoned railroad yard and invited Frank Gehry to design a tower there, a stainless-steel tornado that mimes the limestone rock all around. The Gehry tower rises on land that long ago was part of the Alyscamps. The city is being reborn out of what was once its cemetery.

Maja Hoffmann has transformed the yard, with its vast indoor spaces built to accommodate trains, into a place for exhibitions and invention. She brought landscape artists to reinvent the idea of a great French garden. The tower will become a workplace where creative, ambitious people from around the world will come to make things—new things fashioned out of local resources and regional know-how. Her vision arises from the understanding that we are in a moment of ecological and social transition in which the fate of humanity may be at stake. Survival depends on bringing together the world's expertise to find solutions on which survival may depend—at the beginning of a new millennium. Unlike most French societies, LUMA will focus more on doing than talking, making new things, creating new opportunities for work and living.

In Arles they will constantly feel the urgency to preserve the spirit of the place with every step they take. At dusk the stones of Arles are haunted by the ghosts of three thousand years of human habitation.

But this is Arles, *urbs dupleix*, where nothing goes without contradiction. There are many in Arles who view the tower as a grotesque affront, a sore thumb, or, if you like, a middle finger (*un bras d'honneur*) addressed to the locals. For them, it's another one of those pseudopods by which Parisian globalism extrudes itself into the provinces bringing snobbery, exploitation, and international crowds.

The snobs ill disguise their disdain for the provincials, starting with their twangy accents. The word *bien*, in northern French, with its brief vocalic nasal sound at the end becomes *biaing* in the Midi, because there were no nasal sounds in Provençal, or Old Occitan, a form of which the people spoke for hundreds of years before they began speaking French. There are those in Arles

IX.2. A witty wall in the rue Favorin

who love the sound, the sing-song rhythms of its intonations, the musicality of the final *e*, which is mute in northern French but is generally pronounced in the South, often with significant intimations. "Je t'aim-euh" has three breathy vowels, not two.

Many of the people of Arles cherish the small-town familiarity of local connections, old ways and customs they aren't eager to change. They don't want your crowds, your pretensions, your corporate drug money buying up the city's hotels. They see Hoffmann's LUMA as a familiar form of Parisian colonialism.

Conversely, the Parisians and the local elites see the protests, the grumbling, as evidence of the reactionary reality of the "autochthones," the natives, the indigenous, the aboriginals, who hate "culture" and have a fundamental lack of curiosity. Nothing interests them except what confirms their prejudices, comforts their narratives, extols their local particularities. They are often like what used to be called "*Identitaires*," members of a political movement that appeared first in Europe at the end of the nineteenth century, often allied with the extreme Right, that militates for the defense of its regional identities. For example, people in Provence have made a cult of the highly criticized

IX.3. The Gehry tower, dazzling at dusk

Dr. Raoult from Marseille who claims to cure COVID-19 with the widely discredited hydroxychloroquine. "Raoult, our beacon in the night," "Don't touch our Raoult," they cry in the streets.

Arles might sooner become a city without cults than without conflict. In Arles there will always be two sides to everything: chiffonistes/monnaidiers, Right/Left, reactionary/radical, however much the meaning of those terms may change. It's not even clear, at the moment, which side is Right and which is Left. Seen from the standpoint of the LUMA fans, the local autochthones are knuckle-dragging reactionaries. From the perspective of those attached to their local particularities, the LUMA crowd are corporate globalists who exploit and crush the people. Even I, who has seen it all, can't tell how it will all turn out or even if the doubleness will ever be *aufgehoben*, as Hegelians say, raised up and transcended.

Humanity is at the point where even if it survives in some form or other, after natural or human disasters, what remains may have forgotten its past, may have lost the memories infused in these ancient stones. If Arles were to become a place where humanity invents new modes of existence, it needs to keep the past in mind and not forget to remember the freedoms advanced by the city's greatest minds, my heroes, Favorinus, Ḳalonymus, and Antonelle. They will promote the freedom to think without cults or prescriptions, the freedom to choose to love or to be whatever object or gender you choose, the political freedom that comes from being truly equal before the law without the distinction of disqualifying differences.

And at the ferias, twice a year, the city will still come together to dance in the streets, music everywhere, with wandering bands and so many improvised discotheques (what they call "bodegas") that everyone can dance to the music they love. People will come from all over to see the corrida and celebrate the city in streets perfumed by clouds of anis and the smell of paella cooking outdoors in great flat pans. They will drink glass after glass of the water-fogged sun of golden pastis not in order to forget but to remember how they were at last year's feria and the ones before that.

FIN

Acknowledgments

Favorinus could not exist as a subject of study if it were not for the magnificent work of generations of philologists who devoted their lives to collecting, correcting, and annotating what remains of his writing.

You do not fully appreciate the enormity of the philological undertaking unless you examine a critical edition of his work like the one I have been using, the two volumes prepared by Eugenio Amato: *Favorinus d'Arles*. It is a masterpiece of the genre. It assembles not only the principal texts that remain scattered in different archives but also the fragments of his work that are cited by his contemporaries. In the case of Favorinus, he is quoted, often at length, by some twenty other authors in antiquity. After collecting the totality of texts that can be confidently attributed to him, the philologist must decipher the aged, usually damaged papyrus, restoring lacunae, reconciling different manuscripts, and resolving conflicting interpretations of textual details. The aim is to establish something close to the author's original intention from what remains of papyrus often hastily written by negligent scribes. It is difficult to imagine the fierce patience required to establish a responsible text, the unremitting focus of attention—over years—to the slightest significant detail. It goes without saying that one must be perfectly in command of ancient Greek and Latin.

Preparing a critical edition like this one requires, in addition, that one provide an elaborate system of footnotes to the text signaling every anomaly, elucidating obscurities, identifying people and places. In the case of Favorinus, whose erudition was said by some to be divine, the editor needs hundreds of pages to clarify the myriad references that Favorinus could spontaneously produce on virtually any topic. He had a seemingly total command of Greek and Latin history and legend, literature and philosophy, science and medicine. Because the orator was paid to speak at length, Favorinus was famously prolix; if he mentions one celebrated woman in antiquity, he will immediately name nine others. The poor editor must then provide a footnote for each name, often in elaborate detail.

In the "Avant-propos," Amato modestly announces that his "principal objective" is "to reassemble what remains of the writings of Favorinus" in order "to offer to other scholars a basis for their further research on the rhetoric and culture of the Imperial era." The idea that further research will leave behind Amato's masterpiece, destined to be merely a moment *dépassé* in our understanding, fails to acknowledge how much our further understanding will have been largely anticipated and expressly formulated in the notes and commentary of Amato's modest "basis."

Pierre Serna's brilliant biography, *Antonelle, aristocrate révolutionnaire, 1747–1817*, was the source of practically everything I know about Pierre-Antoine Antonelle. The task of recording his life was infinitely complicated by the way he "seems absent from his own history, from his early years. He is like an empty space, a blank, in a tableau that doesn't otherwise lack for colors."[1] Without passing judgment or resorting to hagiography, Serna displays the extraordinary career of Antonelle (with all his perversions) in meticulous and well-chosen detail. Writing the biography required intense archival work to uncover scattered evidence with which to construct a coherent narrative, particularly because the politics of Antonelle entailed myriad plots and conspiratorial secrets. Nothing frightens Serna when it comes to proposing persuasive solutions to the many enigmas surrounding the career of Antonelle. He exercises immaculate rigor and modesty in presenting alternative interpretations of the biography.

Serna not only has a vast understanding of the period of the French Revolution; he is also thoroughly informed about recent developments in critical theory, which allows him to open perspectives and raise questions that a conventional historian would not offer.

Throughout the writing of this I was sustained by the praise of Eric Loret, whose impeccable critical judgment and flawless literary taste made me believe I could pull this off.

Fabien Vallos, a great teacher and translator, revealed Favorinus to me.

Agnes Droulers never stopped encouraging me with her bubbling spirit that dispelled many dark moments.

Marie-Anne Devaux created the photos for this book. She's a professional photographer and my oldest friend in France. She has always been my staunchest supporter, and here she has wondrously contributed to the beauty of this book with her loving pictures of Arles.

Maria Finders graciously opened doors for me.

Anne Feinberg Pelligrini pointed me in several important directions in her wonderful Arlesian bookstore, *De natura rerum*.

Susan gave me her love and so much laughter.

Notes

I. Urbs Dupleix

1. Favorinos d'Arles, *Discours aux Corinthiens*, 37.
2. Serna, *Antonelle*, 82.
3. Petition, signed by thirty citizens of Arles, requesting that Mayor Jacques Tardieu have Van Gogh committed, shortly before February 27, 1889 (ACA). Probably drawn up by François Damase Crévoulin, the first signatory. Reproduced in Van Gogh exhibition catalog (Amsterdam, 2016), 145.
4. Philostratus, *Life of the Sophists*, 1:viii.
5. Martial, *Epigrams*, 84.
6. Martial, *Epigrams*, 84.
7. Aulus Gellius, *Attic Nights*, 3.

II. Quid Obstat Fit in Via

1. Aulus Gellius, *Attic Nights*, 8.
2. Favorinus d'Arles, *L'Exil*, 17–18.
3. Rouquette, *Arles*, 247.
4. Caesarius, *Regula ad Virgines*.
5. Peter Damian, *Book of Gomorrah*, Letter 31.

III. Colonia Julia Paterna Arelate

1. Avienus, "*Ora Maritima.*"
2. Caesar, *Commentaries on the Civil War*, 3:93–94.
3. Favorinos d'Arles, *Discours aux Corinthiens*.
4. Lucian, *Works of Lucian of Samosata*, 1:632.
5. Rouquette, *Arles: Histoire, territoires et cultures*, 31.

IV. Venus Genetrix

    1. Lamartine, *Cours familier de littérature*, 7:239.

V. Urbs Genesii

    1. Gibbon, *Decline and Fall of the Roman Empire*.
    2. St. Augustine, *Confessions of St. Augustine*, book 6.
    3. Dante, *Inferno*, canto IX.
    4. Klein, "Mêtis of Centaurs."
    5. Klein, "Oxymorons of Anxiety."

VI. Peri Tuché

    1. Aulus Gellius, *Attic Nights*, xii.
    2. Aulus Gellius, *Attic Nights*, 9.
    3. Jaeger, *Paideia*, 115–35.
    4. Aulus Gellius, *Attic Nights*, 293.
    5. Tertullian, *Apology*, chap. 2.
    6. St. Paul, 1 Corinthians 2 (Gideons).

VII. Felix Carcar

    1. Zosimus, *New History*.
    2. Cyprian, *Treatise 1*, 586.
    3. Paul VI, *Evangelii nuntiandi*.
    4. Zosimus, *New History*, vol. 2.
    5. "Mythbusting Ancient Rome: Did Christians Ban the Ancient Olympics?," Ancient Origins, February 22, 2018, www.ancient-origins.net/history-ancient-traditions/mythbusting-ancient-rome-did-christians-ban-ancient-olympics-009632.

VIII. A Worthy Woman: [אשה הגונה]

    1. Eusebius, *Vita Constantini*, 246.
    2. Luke 19:27 (Gideons).
    3. Chrysostom, *Discourses against Judaizing Christians*.
    4. Caesarius, *Regula ad Virgines*.
    5. Gregory I, "Gregory the Great and the Jews."
    6. Ḳalonymus ben Ḳalonymus, *Animals' Lawsuit against Humanity*.
    7. Freud, *Standard Edition*, 22:132.
    8. Vidal, "Ab l'alen tir vas me l'aire."
    9. Ḳalonymus ben Ḳalonymus, *Sefer Even Boḥan*, n.p.

IX. A Republic of Equals

1. Serna, *Antonelle*, 49.
2. Serna, *Antonelle*, 74.
3. Baudelaire, "L'Héautontimorouménos," 78.
4. Serna, *Antonelle*, 82.
5. Serna, *Antonelle*, 87.
6. Serna, *Antonelle*, 57.
7. Serna, *Antonelle*, 84.
8. Serna, *Antonelle*, 81.
9. Serna, *Antonelle*, 123.
10. Serna, *Antonelle*, 123.
11. Serna, *Antonelle*, 134.
12. Serna, *Antonelle*, 140.
13. Serna, *Antonelle*, 142.
14. Serna, *Antonelle*, 219.
15. Serna, *Antonelle*, 247.
16. Serna, *Antonelle*, 291.
17. Serna, *Antonelle*, 253.
18. Serna, *Antonelle*, 293.
19. Serna, *Antonelle*, 287.
20. Serna, *Antonelle*, 433–34.

Acknowledgments

1. Serna, *Antonelle*, 33.

Bibliography

Amato, Eugenio. *Favorinus d'Arles, Oeuvres*. 3 tomes. Translated by Yvette Julien. Paris: Les Belles Lettres, 2005.

Athanassiadi, Polymnia. *Vers la pensée unique: la montée de l'intolérance dans l'Antiquité tardive*. Paris: Les Belles Lettres, 2018.

Augustine of Hippo, Saint. *The Confessions of St. Augustine*. Translated by John K. Ryan. New York: Image Books, 1960.

Aulus Gellius. *Attic Nights of Aulus Gellius*. Translated by John C. Rolfe. Cambridge, MA: Harvard University Press, 1998.

Avienus, Rufius Festus. "*Ora maritima.*" In *The Concise Oxford Dictionary of Archaeology*, edited by Timothy Darvil, 75. Oxford: Oxford University Press, 2002.

Baudelaire, Charles. "L'Héautontimorouménos." In *Les Fleurs du mal, Oeuvres complètes*, 78. Paris: Éditions Gallimard, 1975.

Bernard, Jean-Marc, and Hervé Hôte. *Arles, décor et sculpture*. Arles: Éditions Honoré Clair, 2009.

Brunaux, Jean-Louis. *Vercingétorix*. Paris: Éditions Gallimard, 2018.

Caesar, Gaius Julius. *De Bello Gallico*. Columbia, SC: Pukka Classic, 2018.

Caesarius, Saint. *Regula ad Virgines*. In Césare d'Arles, *Sermons au peuple*, translated by Marie-José Delage. Paris: Éditions du Cerf, 1971.

Caylux, Odile. *Les hotels particuliars d'Arles*. Arles: Actes Sud, 2000.

Chuvin, Pierre. *Chronique des derniers païens: la disparition du paganism dans l'Empire romain, du règne de Constantin à celui de Justinien*. Paris: Les Belles Lettres, Fayard, 2011.

Chrysostom, John. *Discourses against Judaizing Christians*. Translated by Paul W. Harkins. Washington, DC: Catholic University of America Press, 1979.

Cyprian, Saint. *Treatise 1*. In *The Complete Works of Saint Cyprian of Carthage*, edited by Phillip Campbell, 586. New Jersey: Evolution Publishing, 2013.

Eusebius. *Eusebius Pamphilus: Life of Constantine*. Vol. 1 of *The Nicene and Post-Nicene Fathers of the Christian Church*, 2nd series. Translated by Philip Schaff and Henry Wace. Grand Rapids, MI: Wm. B. Eerdman's, 1995.

Favorinos d'Arles. "Discours aux Corinthiens." In Amato, ed., *Oeuvres. Tome 1*, 385–413. Paris: Les Belles Lettres, 2010.

Favorinos d'Arles. *Le traité Sur l'exil de Favorinos d'Arles: papyrologie, philologie et littérature*. Edited by Eugenio Amato and translated by Marie-Hélène Marganne. Rennes, France: Presses Universitaires de Rennes, 2015.

Favorinus d'Arles. *L'Exil*. Translated by Fabien Vallos. Paris: Éditions Mix, 2019.

Freud, Sigmund. *The Standard Edition of the Complete Psychological Works of Sigmund Freud. Vol. 22: New Introductory Lectures on Psycho-analysis and Other Works*. Translated and edited by James Strachey in collaboration with Anna Freud, assisted by Alix Strachey and Alan Tyson. London: Hogarth Press, 1939.

Gauthier, Jean. *Le Coureur du Soleil*. Anglet, France: Atlantica, 2004.

Gibbon, Edward. *The Decline and Fall of the Roman Empire*. New York: Heritage Press, 1946.

Gleason, Maud W. *Making Men: Sophists and Self-Presentation in Ancient Rome*. Princeton, NJ: Princeton University Press, 1995.

Golvin, Jean-Claude, and Gérard Coulon. *Voyage en Gaul Romaine*. Arles, France: Actes Sud, 2016.

Gregory I, Pope. "Gregory the Great and the Jews, 590–604." In Jacob Rader Marcus, *The Jew in the Medieval World: A Source Book, 315–1791*, 124–27. New York: Hebrew Union College Press, 2000.

Jaeger, Werner. *Early Christianity and Greek Paideia*. Cambridge, MA: Harvard University Press, 1985.

Jaeger, Werner. *Paideia: The Ideals of Greek Culture*. Vol. 1. Translated from the second German edition by Gilbert Highet. New York: Oxford University Press, 1986.

Ḳalonymus ben Ḳalonymus. *The Animal's Lawsuit against Humanity*. Translated and adapted by Anson Laytner and Dan Bridge. Louisville, KY: Fons Vitae, 2022.

Ḳalonymus ben Ḳalonymus ben Meir. *Sefer Even Boḥan* (Touchstone). https://archive .org/details/EvenBohanKalonymusbenKalonymusbenMeir1544.

Klein, Richard. "The Mētis of Centaurs." *Diacritics* 16, no. 2 (1986): 2–13.

Klein, Richard. "Oxymorons of Anxiety." *Diacritics* 40, no. 4 (2012): 6–22.

Lamartine, Alphonse de. *Cours familier de littérature: un entretien par mois*. Vol. 7. Paris: Printed for the author, 1856–69. Project Gutenberg, 2012. https://www .gutenberg.org/ebooks/41054.

Legré, Ludovic. *Favorin d'Arles, sa vie, ses oeuvres, ses contemporains*. Marseille, France: Barlatier-Feissat Père et Fils, 1878.

Long, Luc, and Pascal Picard. *César, le Rhône pour mémoire: vingt ans de fouilles archéologiques dans le fleuve à Arles*. Arles, France: Actes Sud, 2009.

Lucian. *The Works of Lucian of Samosata*. Translated by Henry Watson Fowler and Francis George Fowler. Rennes, France: Presse Universitaire de Rennes, 2015.

Martial. *Epigrams*. Vol. 1. Cambridge, MA: Harvard University Press, 1993.

Nouss, Alexis. *La condition de l'exilé: penser les migrations contemporaines.* Paris: Les Editions de la Maison des sciences de l'homme, 2015.

Omrani, Bijan. *Caesar's Footprints.* New York: Pegasus, 2017.

Pascal, Odile, and Magali Pascal. *Histoire du costume d'Arles.* Arles, France: Editions du C.R.C., 2001.

Paul VI, Pope. *Evangelii nuntiandi.* The Vatican: Libreria Editrice Vaticana, 1975.

Peter Damian, Saint. *The Book of Gomorrah and St. Peter Damian's Struggle against Ecclesiatical Corruption.* Translated by Matthew Cullinan Hoffman. New Braunfels, Texas: IABTM Publications, 2015.

Philostratus. *Life of the Sophists.* In *Philostratus, "Life of the Sophists" and Eunapius, "Lives of Philosophers and Sophists, 4–148."* Translated by Han Baltussen and Graeme Miles. Cambridge, MA: Harvard University Press, 2023.

Pichot, Amédée. *Le dernier roi d'Arles: épisode des grandes chroniques arlésiennes comprenant les légendes du Lion, du Cheval et de la Tarasque, etc., etc., précédé d'un essai historique sur la ville d'Arles, depuis son origine jusqu'à ce jour.* Paris: Palala Press, 2016.

Privat, Eduard, ed. *Juifs at judaisme de Languedoc.* Fanjeaux, France: Centre d'études historiques de Fanjeaux, 1977.

Rouquette, Jean-Maurice, ed. *Arles: Histoire, territoires et cultures.* Paris: Imprimerie nationale Editions, 2008.

Rouquette, Jean-Maurice, Patrick Blanc, Veronique Blanc, Jacques Bremond, Alain Charron, Marc Heijmans, Michel Lacanaud, et al. *Musée de l'Arles antique.* Arles, France: Actes Sud, 1996.

Schama, Simon. *The Story of the Jews: Finding the Words, 1000 BC–1492 AD.* New York: HarperCollins, 2013.

Sérena-Allier, Dominique. *Louis XIV et la Vénus d'Arles: la plus belle femme de ma royaume.* Arles, France: Actes Sud, 2013.

Serna, Pierre. *Antonelle, aristocrate révolutionnaire, 1747–1817.* Paris: Éditions du Félin, 1997.

Tertullian. *Apology.* Cambridge, MA: Harvard University Press, 1931.

Tomer, Jerry. *The Day Commodus Killed a Rhino: Understanding the Roman Games.* Baltimore: Johns Hopkins University Press, 2014.

Ulansay, David. *The Origins of the Mithraic Mysteries: Cosmology and Salvation in the Ancient World.* Oxford: Oxford University Press, 1989.

Van Nuffelen, Peter. *Penser la tolérance durant l'Antiquité tardive.* Paris: Les Éditions du Cerf, 2018.

Vidal, Peire. "Ab l'alen tir vas me l'aire." In Martín de Riquer, *Los trovadores: historia literaria y textos,* tomo 2, 872–73. Barcelona: Editorial Ariel, 1975.

Zosimus the Historian. *The New History.* 2 vols. Edited by Taylor Anderson. CreateSpace, 2017.